ORGANISATION DESIGN

Better Management Skills

This highly popular range of inexpensive paperbacks covers all areas of basic management. Practical, easy to read and instantly accessible, these guides will help managers to improve their business or communication skills. Those marked * are available on audio cassette.

The books in this series can be tailored to specific company requirements. For further details, please contact the publisher, Kogan Page, telephone 0171 278 0433, fax 0171 837 6348.

ORGANISATION DESIGN

A GUIDE FOR TEAM LEADERS, BUSINESS OWNERS AND CHANGE MANAGERS

**MARGARET R DAVIS
AND DAVID A WECKLER**

KOGAN PAGE
BETTER MANAGEMENT SKILLS

First published in the United States of America in 1996, entitled *A Practical Guide to Organization Design*, by Crisp Publications Inc, 1200 Hamilton Court, Menlo Park, California 94025, USA.

This edition first published in Great Britain in 1997 by Kogan Page Ltd, 120 Pentonville Road, London N1 9JN.

British Library Cataloguing in Publication Data

A CIP record for this book is available from the British Library.

ISBN 0-7494-2445-1

Typeset by BookEns Ltd, Royston, Herts.
Printed in England by Clays Ltd, St Ives plc

Contents

Introduction

This book is about organisation design. *Organisation design* is the planning and fitting together of the people and activities involved in doing the work of an organisation. It includes creating the 'boxes and lines' of an organisation chart and finding ways to make sure that the right work gets done the right way — with the desired results.

An *organisation* is any collection of people and activities formed for a specific purpose. The world we interact with every day is filled with organisations of all kinds: product manufacturers, retail stores, banks, government agencies, volunteer associations. And there are organisations within organisations: Ford Motor Company is an organisation, and so are the divisions that produce Transit vans, Mondeos and Fiestas. Each department within each division is an 'organisation within an organisation'.

This book was written for anyone who is embarking on the design or redesign of an organisation. The ideas and techniques we present can be used in any organisation: large and small; profit and non-profit; public and private; industrial, professional, government and educational. We give examples and exercises to help you apply the ideas to your own organisation.

If you follow management trends in the news media, you will know that new buzzwords appear at frequent intervals. For example, in recent years, we have heard much about 're-engineering', 'teams', 'total quality management', 'business process improvement', and so on. Many of these approaches add valuable new perspectives to the business of organisation design. But to make any of them work you need to understand the basics of organisation design as we present them here.

First, you need to understand our particular usage of a few key words.

An **organisation** is any collection of people and activities formed for a specific purpose. We use the words *organisation, business, company, corporation, enterprise* and *firm* more or less interchangeably. We do this simply to avoid being repetitious. These ideas apply no matter what kind of organisation you have.

Unit is a generic term used to describe any subdivision of an organisation. Divisions, departments, sections, work groups and teams are all units.

Customer means 'anyone who uses the products or services you provide'. In your business, these people might be called *clients* or *users*, for example, rather than customers.

Stakeholders are all those people or institutions who have an interest in your organisation and who can influence what you do and how successful you are. For a typical business, stakeholders include owners, employees, customers, shareholders, suppliers, regulators and even competitors.

Why does organisation design matter?

Although it is true that the unique personalities of individuals in an organisation influence everything that goes on, it is also true that the 'impersonal' design factors we discuss here have a very powerful impact on shaping people's attitudes and behaviour and on their opportunities and performance on the job. A good design greatly enhances organisational effectiveness; a poor design can, and often does, actively prevent the organisation from being successful.

This brings to mind a dilemma that people often face when they set out to redesign an organisation. That is, to what extent should you focus on building an 'ideal' organisation rather than creating a design that fits the employees and facilities already in place? We suggest you (1) think through what an 'ideal' organisation design would be, (2) see how this fits with your existing resources and (3) do some tweaking to both the design and the people to get a satisfactory resolution. Even if the immediate compromise is a long way from the 'ideal', you will have some ideas of what to aim for in the long run.

Putting organisation design in context

It is worth noting that organisation design is one of four steps in organising or reorganising a business enterprise. The four steps are:

1. Assessing the business situation
- Opportunities and threats
- Resources

2. Developing a business strategy
- Mission, goals
- Key success factors
- Customer needs
- Products, services

3. Organisation design
- Business processes
- Dividing up the work
- Management structure
- Coordination, control, measurement

4. Implementing the new design
- Ongoing monitoring or design effectiveness.

The first step, *assessing the business situation*, consists of scanning the business environment, noting what opportunities and threats exist for the organisation, and what resources are available, or need to be obtained, to compete. Together, these assessments influence the perceived need to change.

This leads to the second step, *developing a business strategy*. This includes reviewing the organisation's mission, setting goals, defining key success factors, determining customer needs and the products and services to offer. Although not the subject of this book, we briefly discuss mission, goals, and success factors in the next chapter because the chances of designing an effective organisation are greater if these issues are clear.

Third, there is the topic of this book, *organisation design*. This step includes describing business processes; deciding how best to split up people and work into units such as divisions, departments and teams; creating a management structure and finding ways to coordinate and control work and to measure results.

Fourth, *implementation* is putting the new design into operation. This is not as final a step as it sounds. In most companies, organisation design is an ongoing process with much rethinking, tweaking and modifying of current arrangements.

When do you need to redesign an organisation?

The purpose of organisation design is to help the organisation use its resources in the best way possible to reach its goals and carry out its business strategies. It is appropriate to reconsider the way your organisation is designed whenever:

- Your organisation is faced with an immediate or anticipated change in its situation – for example, new competition, new markets, new products or services, major changes in technology, a merger with another company – anything that results in new goals and new business strategies.
- For any reason you feel the need to improve organisational performance – for example, to reduce costs, increase profitability or improve quality.

The old adage, 'If it ain't broke, don't fix it', can be highly misleading in today's business world. Technological break-throughs occur frequently, spread quickly and can dramatically alter your formula for success. New opportunities that arise often give you only a brief window of time to react before the competition beats you to it.

Successful companies are constantly responding to any changes they see coming up – in business opportunities, technology, resources, competition, regulation or anything that might affect their business. In fact, it has been said of Hewlett-Packard that they don't wait for a competitor to come out with a better product; instead, they make their own products obsolete *before* their competitors do.

At the same time, major organisation redesigns can be costly, time consuming and demoralising to employees – at least in the short run. Changing the organisation around just for the sake of it is unlikely to bring many benefits. What is beneficial is to make sure on an ongoing basis that your structure and management methods are helping, not hindering, the organisation's success.

Objectives of this book

In writing this book, we have three aims: *first*, to summarise and simplify existing knowledge about organisation design – that is, the rationale for alternative ways of doing things and the strengths and drawbacks of each alternative; *second*, to provide clear guidelines and questions to enable you to apply the ideas to your own case; and, *third*, to do both these things in a way that is useful not only to managers but to everyone in an organisation who may take part in a design process.

Today, more than ever before, employees at all levels are being drawn into task forces, teams, problem-solving groups and other situations where they are asked to give their opinions and help their organisations to be more competitive. This book can help everyone to make a useful contribution.

Questions to ask before getting started

You may be designing a brand-new organisation, revamping an existing one or just making some minor changes in a few areas. Whatever the scope of the design activity, it helps to be as clear as possible on five things.

1. *What are you setting out to do through organisation design?* Is it a complete overhaul of your structure or of just one part, streamlining to cut costs, taking advantage of new technology, improving responsiveness to customers? Being clear on what you're trying to accomplish will help you to focus on the right issues, choose the right people to involve and not wander off at tangents.

2. *How will you know when you have succeeded?* How do you plan to measure success? Through improved customer satisfaction ratings? Fewer product rejects? Less waste? Lower production costs? Reduced headcount? If you know what success is for you, you'll make better decisions throughout the design process.

3. *What stakeholders do you need to satisfy?* How will your key stakeholders be affected by changes you make in the organisation? How can you make changes as easy as possible for them to accept? Keeping these things in mind as you go forward will help to prevent confused or negative reactions afterwards.

4. *What resources do you have?* Your resources include employees – their numbers, skills, experience, knowledge. Resources also include time, money, materials, equipment, facilities and other people or sources of information and help outside your organisation that are available to you.

5. *What barriers or constraints do you face?* A shortage of important resources is one constraint. Others may include laws and government regulations that affect your business, competition, or unwillingness of organisational members to change.

CHAPTER 1
First Steps

Before embarking on organisation design, you must first understand where your organisation is headed – in other words, your mission and goals – and what key factors are required for your success. However, this chapter focuses mainly on *business processes* and the way that work activities are linked to produce products and services for the customer.

Mission and goals

Your mission and goals spell out what your organisation is being designed to do. They are important because, as the saying goes, 'If you don't know where you're going, any road will get you there.'

Mission

An organisation's mission is the reason it exists. Every organisation has a mission, even though it frequently is not spelled out in writing. A written *mission statement* is useful in communicating to the world your reason for existing, and also as a periodic reminder to employees of what you're all about.

A good mission statement:

● Describes your business purpose

- Reflects key customer needs and wants you are satisfying
- Creates the context for goal setting and planning.

Goals

Goals are results you intend to achieve. Your mission states what business you're in. Your goals state the concrete results you aim for within a specified period.

Goals commonly relate to:

- Financial results, such as profit margins, total sales, lower costs of production
- Customer concerns, such as quantity and quality of products and services, turnaround time for orders, cost of products.

To be useful, goals are:

- Measurable — it is clear whether or not they have been achieved
- Realistic — they can be reached in the time stated and with the resources you have
- Challenging — they require you and your co-workers to put forward your best efforts.

As you develop your goals, it's a good idea at the same time to define how you're going to measure success for each one. Sometimes, this is obvious. For example:

Goal: Sell 200 more widgets this year than last.
How to measure: Subtract number of widgets sold last year from number sold this year.

Sometimes, it's not quite this easy.

Goal: Increase customer satisfaction this year.
How to measure: Develop a customer satisfaction survey; administer it at the beginning of the year and again at the end. Compare the results.

Chapter 5 will present more information on ways to measure performance.

Key success factors

Whereas a goal is a specific achievement you are aiming for within a specified period, a key success factor is something you must pay attention to all the time. To identify key success factors for your business, ask yourself: *What must we do to be successful?*

For a profit-making business, success means making a profit. Key success factors would vary depending on how that business makes its profit. For instance: for a business that produces low-cost clothing, key success factors might be having low-cost operations and high-volume sales. For a manufacturer of women's luxury clothing, costs wouldn't be as important as high quality – of material, construction and so on – and creative design.

As you evaluate alternative ways to design your organisation, keep the key success factors in mind. Some design alternatives may clearly be better than others in helping you to be successful.

Business processes

Being clear on mission, goals and key success factors are all preliminary to organisation design. The first step in the design process itself is to identify the work that must be done to produce something of value for your customers and to see how this work is sequenced to form business processes.

What is a business process?
A business process consists of the sequence of tasks and activities that must be completed to provide a product or service to the customer. To identify your business processes, you must ask yourself: What work is necessary to produce our products and services, and how are the tasks and activities linked together? We'll use a simple domestic situation to illustrate.

Say that you want to give a dinner party. The process starts when it occurs to you that you would like to repay the hospitality of several friends. The end result of the process will be a dinner served to your friends.

The steps in the process are as follows:

1. You think, 'I'd like to have a dinner party.'
2. Prepare guest list, decide date and time, send out invitations.
3. Plan menu, select recipes.
4. Prepare grocery list, buy groceries.
5. Clean house.
6. Cook dinner, set table.
7. Guests arrive.
8. Serve dinner.
9. Guests express appreciation.

Obviously, this is a highly simplified version of the whole process. Some steps involve subprocesses. Take 'cook dinner', for example. You'll need to begin preparation of different dishes at different times; some can be prepared in advance, some will need to be cooking while other courses are being served. Each course has its own mix of ingredients, mustn't be over- or undercooked and must be coordinated with all the other courses so that everything is ready to be served at just the right time.

In terms of organisation design:

- *First*, the end result or outcome – dinner on the table – corresponds to the product or service provided to customers.
- *Second*, the overall sequence of steps corresponds to a business process.
- *Third*, the more detailed set of tasks within each major step forms a subprocess.

Why are business processes important?

Probably everyone in an organisation could easily name its major products and services, but many employees would be stumped if they were asked to describe their major business processes. This is because so often the work in a company is compartmentalised, and people in one department often have only a vague idea of how other departments contribute to the same end product. Thinking through each business process can help each individual to understand where and how their work fits into the overall picture.

Not only does this make work more meaningful to the average employee, but when everyone understands the ultimate point of what they are doing, it's easier for them to see how to make their part, as well as the overall product or service, more satisfying to the customer. It may also help employees to see where a process can be made more efficient or even come up with new products and services.

Another reason it's important to understand your business processes is that this knowledge will guide you through the stages of organisation design that follow. We'll return to this point later in the chapter.

Describing business processes

In thinking through the steps in a business process, it's helpful to think in terms of *end, start* and *in-between*. That is, start with the end result – the product or service that the process leads to. Next, note what step starts the process, and then identify each step in between. Consider the Enlok Windows example, illustrated in Figure 1.1.

Enlok Windows manufactures and installs custom-designed windows in industrial buildings. One of its business processes involves window replacement in existing industrial buildings. (The process for providing windows for a new building is quite different.)

The *end result* is custom-designed windows that are installed at industrial sites to replace existing windows. The *starting point* is when the customer calls the sales office, explains the requirements, and asks for an estimate of cost. The *in-between* steps are items 2 to 9 on the figure.

Note that every step has its own outcome. For the salesperson, the sales order is an outcome; the estimator's final estimate is an outcome; the same is true of the engineer's drawings; the factory assembler's finished assembly; and so on. However, it is critical to the organisation as a whole to understand that each of these interim outcomes is part of one process and that no one's work is

Start

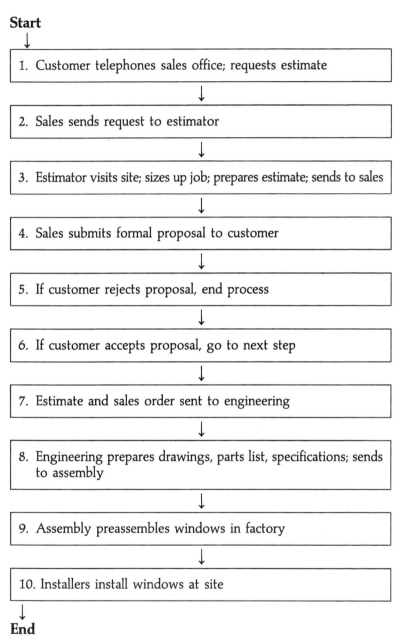

1. Customer telephones sales office; requests estimate

2. Sales sends request to estimator

3. Estimator visits site; sizes up job; prepares estimate; sends to sales

4. Sales submits formal proposal to customer

5. If customer rejects proposal, end process

6. If customer accepts proposal, go to next step

7. Estimate and sales order sent to engineering

8. Engineering prepares drawings, parts list, specifications; sends to assembly

9. Assembly preassembles windows in factory

10. Installers install windows at site

End

Figure 1.1. *Enlok Windows business process: filling customer order for replacement windows*

truly done until the final product is installed at the customer's site to the customer's satisfaction.

You can see how this process view of work departs from the view still prevailing in many organisations that can be summarised as: 'My piece of work is done. I've passed it on to the next one along the line, and it's now his responsibility.'

As mentioned earlier, this is only one business process for Enlok. Another key one for them is filling orders for windows in new industrial buildings. In the second process, because an order may tie up a lot of Enlok's resources, the managing director may have to approve the decision to accept it. Also, in these cases, the customer's architect generally provides the specifications and drawings, and new parts often have to be ordered from outside suppliers. It is a very different process from the first one.

Subprocesses

Earlier, we mentioned that each major step in a process will have one or more subprocesses associated with it. Take, for example, the subprocess that involves the estimator at Enlok (see Figure 1.2).

The *end result* is that the estimate of time and cost is submitted to sales. The *starting point* is when the sales representative notifies the estimator of a customer's request. The *in-between* steps are those that occur between these two points. Subprocesses can be broken down for each task or position involved in a key process.

Workflow charting

A very useful technique to use when you're trying to improve a process is workflow charting. This involves expanding each process and subprocess to show in detail every task and activity in that process. Workflow charts often list not only the activity and sequence, but also who is involved at each step, length of time to complete each activity, the *inputs* (resources, information, and so on) fed into each step and the *outputs* of each step.

This level of detail can be extremely valuable in discovering how things are actually done and finding opportunities for

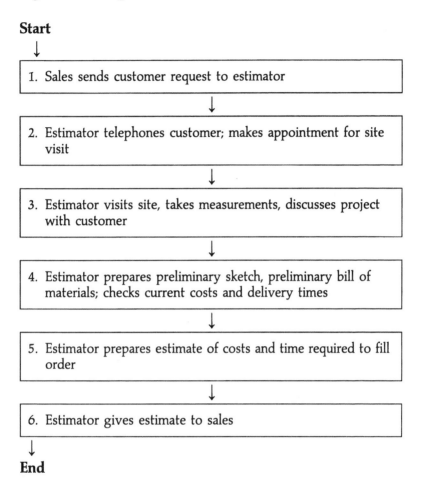

Start

1. Sales sends customer request to estimator

2. Estimator telephones customer; makes appointment for site visit

3. Estimator visits site, takes measurements, discusses project with customer

4. Estimator prepares preliminary sketch, preliminary bill of materials; checks current costs and delivery times

5. Estimator prepares estimate of costs and time required to fill order

6. Estimator gives estimate to sales

End

Figure 1.2. *Enlok Windows subprocess: preparing estimate for replacement windows*

improvement. For example, you might find that some tasks can be combined, or some steps eliminated altogether, or work can be speeded up by changing the sequence of activities.

This level of detail is not usually necessary for the purpose of organisation design. It is important, however, to understand the main business processes and major subprocesses, because this information will be helpful when you go through the design steps in the next chapters.

Core and non-core processes

A *core business process* is one that is directly related to the organisation's mission. *Non-core processes* may still be important but they aren't directly related to the mission.

> *Enlok Windows' mission is to design, assemble and install custom-made windows. The processes for filling customer orders, whether for new buildings or replacement windows, are thus core business processes. Enlok has a human resources department whose function is to make sure the company has a qualified workforce and to serve the needs of that workforce. This function is not directly related to the company's mission, and so the process through which human resources delivers its services is a non-core process.*

Some companies make a deliberate decision to use external contractors for non-core work. Examples of work commonly contracted out include secretarial services, reprographics, artwork and building maintenance. Some companies even eliminate the need for a human resources department by hiring contract employees from employment agencies, which act as the employer: hiring and screening the employees, paying them, administering benefits, and so on. But most companies perform at least some non-core functions in-house.

Even though non-core work processes being and end within the company, it is critical that the people involved understand that the ultimate aim of internal processes is to support the company in serving customers. In some cases, staff programmes appear to become ends in themselves, and their connection to customer service is lost.

The underlying goal of any internal programme is, or should be, to enable the company to serve customers better. If the programme gets in the way of serving customers, then the programme must change.

Business processes and organisation design

Once you have spelled out your business process, you will have essential information to use in designing your organisation. For example, you will be able to see where steps in the work of your organisation are interdependent and, therefore, where coordination and communication are especially important.

Interdependence is the extent to which two or more steps or tasks depend on each other. For example, the end result of one step is required for the next step to begin or to be completed. Or a mistake made in one step will lead to flawed results in the next step too.

Coordination is the linking together of different steps or tasks to produce the intended outcome.

To return to our dinner party example on page 16, groceries can't be purchased (4) until the menu is planned (3), nor can dinner be prepared (6) until the groceries have been purchased. These *interdependencies* mean that these activities must be sequenced in a certain way. On the other hand, cleaning the house (5) could happen at any time.

If other people were helping you with the party arrangements, then *coordination* would become important. You would need to communicate with one another to make sure that nothing slips between the cracks and that you don't duplicate each other's work.

Remember the Enlok Windows example (Figure 1.1). Although all the steps are interdependent to some degree, some are much more so than others.

The second and third steps are not strongly interdependent. Sales give a customer request to the estimator (2), who then prepares the estimate (3). The estimator does not depend on sales to get the information he needs for the estimate – rather, he contacts the customer himself, personally visits the site, and takes measurements.

If, instead, the estimator completely relied on information given to him by sales, there would indeed be high interdependence between these two steps. Sales' ability to submit a formal proposal to the customer (4) is, of course, highly dependent on the results of the estimator's work.

As you can see, interdependence increases the need for

coordination, which often depends on communication. Describing your business processes will illuminate where you need coordination, and this information will help you to assess how good your organisation design is.

It makes sense to have your business needs determine your structure rather than have your structure dictate how work is coordinated. In other words, 'form should follow function'. Ideally, activities that demand close coordination should be located near one another in the organisation – if not physically, at least in the sense of being in the same organisational unit. Whether or not this is possible, the communication and coordination needs of interdependent activities should be designed into the organisation, rather than left to chance.

Guidelines for identifying business processes

Focus initially on your core business processes. The number of these will depend on the size of your organisation and the number of products and services you provide. If the organisation you're designing is a staff support unit within a larger organisation, your business process or processes will probably be non-core. The important point is to see the connection between these non-core processes and the core business processes so that they all serve the ultimate goals of the whole organisation. Each process will undoubtedly break down into a number of subprocesses, which you may find useful to examine in more detail.

Who should be involved?
● *Top level management.* In small to middle-sized companies, the chief executive of the organisation, together with the executives who report to him or her, would undoubtedly be able to name their major business processes and the steps within each. The larger an organisation becomes, however, the more difficult it is for a limited number of even top people to be able to do this.

- *Employees who represent each major step in the process.* The more detail you're trying to capture, the more likely it is you'll want to involve the people who are closest to the work. They are most likely to understand the process that is *actually* followed in addition to the process that is *supposed* to be followed.

The first step is to identify your customers and the products and/ or services you provide to each. Next, name the main process that results in each product or service. Then for each process list every major step needed to accomplish the desired result.

An example of a worksheet format you might use follows. After going through the steps, it may be useful for you to illustrate each business process and major subprocess. The simplest kind of diagram is the block flowchart, such as those already given in this chapter. Simply write out the steps, draw a box around each, and place them in sequence, with arrows to show the direction of flow.

Worksheet

1. **Who are your customers – those people who use the products and services you provide? What product and/ or service do you provide to each?**

   Customer   Product/Service

   _____

   _____

   _____

2. **Identify the major steps in the business process that results in each product or service.**

   First business process: _____

   Product/Service:_____

   First step:_____

Second step:_____

Third step: _____

And so on to last step

Second business process: _____

    Product/Service: _____

    First step: _____

    Second step:_____

    Third step: _____

    And so on to last step

Repeat these steps for all business processes.
Next, list the steps for all necessary subprocesses.

3. **Does it make sense to combine some of these processes?** (For example, you may have two quite different products that are produced through the same process.) If so, which ones?

_____

_____

_____

4. **If you haven't involved many other people in plotting out these processes, you may wish to get their input now on your findings.**

First business process   People to involve/Their input

_____

_____

_____

_____

Second business process   People to involve/Their input

_____

_____

_____

_____

5. **If your organisation is a department that provides internal services only, add this additional question:**

   How do our non-core work processes contribute to the company's core business processes?

_____

_____

_____

You will be returning to this information on business processes when you come to make decisions on dividing up the work, forming a management structure and selecting coordination and control techniques.

CHAPTER 2
Dividing Up the Work

Once you have a good understanding of your mission and goals, the key success factors for your business and the core business processes through which you deliver products and services to customers, it is time to decide what kind of organisation structure is best for you.

This chapter describes five types of organisation structure:

1. Functional
2. Product- or service-based
3. Customer- or geographical-area based
4. Business process teams
5. Matrix.

Organisation structure refers to the way work is divided up. To put it simply, structure is what the boxes and lines on the typical organisation chart represent. The boxes show how work and responsibilities are clustered into units such as divisions, departments, sections and teams. The lines show the management structure – that is, who reports to whom or how the boxes relate to one another in the hierarchy. We discuss boxes in this chapter and lines in Chapter 3.

Why structure matters

The larger the number of task to be done and the more people who are involved, the more important it is to split up work and workers into groups or units such as divisions, departments and teams. There are different ways to do this, and the structure you end up with makes a big difference in terms of:

- What employees pay attention to
- The ease of coordinating activities
- The speed of producing goods
- The cost of running the business
- The nature and extent of supervision required
- Whom employees interact and build relationships with.

In short, the structure of your organisation can make all the difference to your ability to serve customers and stay in business.

Different kinds of structure

As we just mentioned, there are five basic ways to structure an organisation – that is, around function performed, product or service, customers or geographical area served, business process and matrix. Many variations and combinations can be found. Large organisations are almost always *hybrids*, with one type of structure at the top level of the company and others at lower levels.

Each type of structure has relative strengths and drawbacks. Each one might be a good alternative in some situations and a poor alternative in others.

We will use the case of a hypothetical printing company, 'ABC Printing', to illustrate the first four of the five structures.

ABC Printing produces letterheads, envelopes, brochures and business cards. It has a sales force, a staff of graphic designers and a print shop. It sells to large corporations, small businesses and individuals throughout the country and has a small international business.

Functional structure

In a functional structure, units such as divisions and departments are formed according to the major technical or professional function performed by the unit.

If ABC Printing had a functional structure, its departments would be Sales, Graphic Design and Print Shop. Each department would handle all products for both individual and corporate accounts, domestic and overseas.

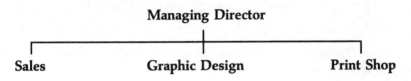

Figure 2.1. *Functional structure for ABC Printing*

Strengths of a functional structure

- It is easier to manage work *within* the group because supervisors and subordinates share the same job-related knowledge.

  ABC's graphic design manager was himself a graphic designer; thus, the schedules and standards he sets are realistic, and he can easily evaluate how well each designer is performing.

- Each group also contains people who 'speak the same language' and who share and nurture one another's technical expertise. This kind of structure tends to attract and develop experts in each functional speciality. In businesses whose success depends on technical expertise, gathering and increasing that expertise can be an important competitive advantage.

  In ABC's case, the designers will tend to gain a lot of technical expertise by interacting with one another. The more people there are in this department and the more varied their skills, the more this will be true. This concentration of talent could be critical to ABC's success.

- Labour costs are often lower than in any of the alternatives we describe because people working on the same kind of task are in one 'pool' — and workload can be more easily balanced as demand rises and falls for different products and different skills.

Drawbacks of a functional structure

- Often you need more than one department to complete a job. In these cases, coordination and communication between departments may be slower and less accurate than desirable. Misunderstandings may arise between departments that are responding to different pressures.

  For example, ABC's salesperson may promise a customer a delivery date that the print shop can't meet.

- Because the involvement of all departments is needed to fill every customer order, each individual department manager has limited decision-making authority.

  ABC's sales manager typically won't be able to authorise an unusual request from a customer without getting approval from the design and print shop managers.

- It may be difficult to develop new ways of doing business, especially if the new business requires unfamiliar cooperation across functional boundaries.

  For example, at ABC Printing, new computer technology may enable the print shop to do graphic design. If organised functionally, these two departments may resist the indicated change and miss early opportunities to compete.

- Different departments will tend to have different priorities. Attempts to resolve conflicts between departments may be costly to the company in terms of time and money and may result in the customers' interests being overlooked.

  Sales may be most concerned about speed of delivery, graphic design about quality of artwork regardless of the time involved, and the print shop about keeping costs low and having a steady flow of work.

- In this structure, it is often difficult to pinpoint accountability for results because each department can simply pass the buck to another.

If a customer complains about the product, sales may claim that graphic design did not interpret the sales order correctly, design may claim that the print shop misunderstood the specifications, and the print shop may claim that it was given an unrealistic deadline.

- Finally, because this kind of structure tends to develop managers who specialise in a particular area, it is not as effective at developing all-round general managers who might be able to run the whole operation.

If ABC's general manager were to leave the company, it would be difficult to promote any one of the three functional managers to this position because their experience is in only one function. For example, the print shop manager does not have skills and experience in graphic design or sales.

Points to ponder

It is important to understand that these potential drawbacks can be lessened or even overcome. For example, if you had a functional structure, how might you:

1. Fend off any tendency to shift the blame among managers of different functions?
2. Develop general management skills in your functional managers?
3. Make sure that the different departments pull together to serve the customers' needs or take advantage of new technology?

Product- or service-based structure

With this alternative, the organisation forms departments or divisions around each of its products or services. Each department or division performs all the functions needed to produce its particular product or service.

So for ABC Printing, there would be a Stationery Division (letterheads and envelopes), a Brochures Division and a Business Cards Division. Each division has its own sales staff, graphic design staff and print shop for individual, corporate, domestic and overseas customers.

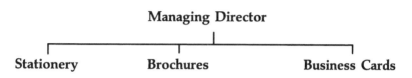

Figure 2.2. *Product-based structure for ABC Printing*

Strengths of a product- or service-based structure

- Responsibility for each product can be pinpointed at the division level.

If a customer is not satisfied with an order for brochures, the brochure division manager is responsible; he or she cannot blame another manager.

- Because everyone in a division focuses on just one product, that product is likely to be of higher quality, or more state of the art, than products in a multiproduct division.

If ABC has a division that focuses on brochures only, it is more likely to become a 'leading edge' brochure producer than if those employees spread their efforts among all the company's products.

- A team spirit will develop around each product line, and competition among divisions or departments can boost business all around.

At ABC, the stationery and brochures divisions may compete to get the most customers, the highest gross sales, or the highest profit margin, thus making the company as a whole more successful.

- A good candidate pool for top management can be developed, because each division manager will learn to manage several functions and will probably have more independence in making decisions.

  For example, ABC's brochures manager will be adept at managing sales, graphic design and a print shop.

- Because division managers will have some independence in making decisions, they can respond more quickly to customer requests.

  If a customer wanted an especially large format brochure, the ABC brochures manager could decide on his own whether or not to accept this order without having to wait for approval from the other managers.

Drawbacks of a product- or service-based structure

- There may be less sharing of resources across divisions and more duplication of effort, with resulting higher costs.

  With this structure, ABC would end up with three groups of sales people, three groups of graphic designers and three print shops — one for each product line.

- Career opportunities may be restricted somewhat for professionals because their experience will be limited to just one product line.

  For example, designers in the stationery division won't get experience in designing business cards or brochures.

- Customers who want multiple products and services will have to work with more than one division.

  ABC's customers who want coordinated graphics in brochures, stationery and business cards will have to work with three different divisions.

- Because each division is an advocate for its own particular product, the company may be slow to recognise that a product should be changed, dropped or added.

The stationery division manager may urge the company to retain that product line even if it is no longer profitable.

Customer- or geographical area-based structure

In this alternative, the organisation structures its major units around the characteristics or location of its customers or markets.

If ABC Printing were organised this way, it would have separate divisions to handle large corporate accounts, small businesses and individual accounts; or it might divide up geographically, with separate divisions to serve home market customers, European and overseas customers. Each division would handle all products and have its own sales, design and printing staff but would serve only one type *of account or service area.*

Managing Director

Corporate Accounts	Individual Accounts	Overseas Accounts
Home Market	Home Market	Corporate

Figure 2.3. *Customer-based structure for ABC Printing*

Strengths of a customer-based structure

● The unique needs of each type of customer are well served. The orientation of the company will be to meet customer needs.

For ABC, product and marketing requirements are likely to be quite different overseas as compared with the domestic market. There may be different language requirements and different cultural factors to consider. Corporate clients will require different credit arrangements and pricing from retail customers.

● The focus on customer or market keeps the company aware

of changes in customers' needs and preferences, especially as compared with the product-based structure.

- Unprofitable product lines are more likely to be dropped than would be the case with either a functional- or product-based structure.

Drawbacks of a customer-based structure

- As with product-based structures, there may be less sharing of resources across division and department boundaries and more duplication of efforts, resulting in higher costs.
- Internal systems may evolve in different ways to serve different customer segments. This may make overall management of the organisation difficult.

For example, ABC might set up different accounting or inventory systems to handle its overseas customers and domestic customers, and this might make it difficult to compare the results of the two market segments.

Points to ponder

If you had an organisation that was structured according to product or customer, how might you overcome some of the potential drawbacks? For example:

1. How can you avoid having experts in each product department if it isn't cost effective to do this? (*Hint:* Consider a hybrid structure with both product-based and functional departments.)
2. How can you make sure that professionals in the organisation don't become too narrowly focused in one product area?
3. How can you make sure that product managers who are basically competing with one another work as a team to serve customers who require more than one kind of product?

Business process team structure

Teams have always been used by organisations to accomplish special, often temporary, projects. Today they are a well-established way of getting work done and can be found in all types of organisation. Cross-functional teams are often given responsibility for complex assignments that fall outside the scope of the traditional departmental structure.

Teams are especially useful:

- When there is a need for flexibility and/or speed in handling projects such as special customer requests, product development or marketing campaigns.
- When it is important to have input from different parts of the organisation simultaneously in completing a piece of work.

In Chapter 1, we discussed business processes and how important it is for everyone in an organisation to understand the steps in each process. In recent years, some companies have begun to structure their organisations, or parts of them, around ongoing business process teams.

The business process team is characteristic of what is sometimes called a 'horizontal organisation', which has been in the limelight a great deal in recent years.

A *horizontal organisation* is one that structures work around its major work processes. It is called horizontal because the work units cut across traditional functions, rather than relying on a vertical hierarchy to coordinate activity. A business process team includes people who can perform all the major activities within a business process so that the members of a single team can collectively carry out the whole process from beginning to end.

In horizontal organisations, the focus is on whatever is involved in completing the work to satisfy customers. This kind of structure tends to reduce the number of levels of management. (It becomes a 'flat' structure, as we describe in Chapter 3.)

Two core business processes for ABC Printing are filling orders for brochures for the domestic market and filling stationery orders for corporate accounts. If ABC were organised by business process, they would have a team (or teams) devoted to each of these processes. Each team would include people with skills in sales, graphic design and printing. The team would handle every step of the process from receipt of initial customer order to delivery of the completed order to the customer.

Note that in each team shown in Figure 2.4, the sales, design and print shop members work as a team with their team leader handling only one kind of product for one customer type. Thus, their work is highly focused.

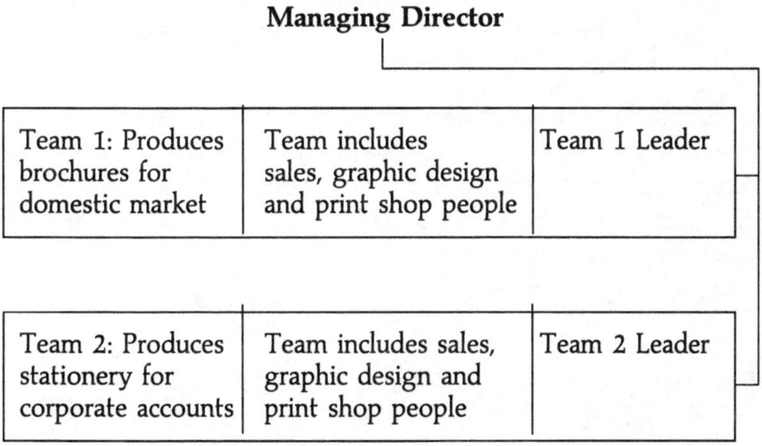

Managing Director

Team 1: Produces brochures for domestic market	Team includes sales, graphic design and print shop people	Team 1 Leader

Team 2: Produces stationery for corporate accounts	Team includes sales, graphic design and print shop people	Team 2 Leader

Figure 2.4. *Business process team structure for ABC Printing*

The teams report directly to the MD. In a large company, it is likely there will be several brochure teams and several stationery teams, which may report to a brochures or stationery manager. Also, these teams have no technical support available within the company. In large companies, it is likely that there would be some design and printing experts to assist them.

Strengths of a business process team structure

- The focus of the organisation is *outwards to customers*, rather than *inwards to a boss*.

- Time, and hence money, are saved because of the reduced need to pass information up and down the hierarchy and between departments.

  For example, if a customer wants an order changed, the request would go to the team who would handle the request by itself. All the people who need to make decisions about the request are on the team.

- Business process teams promote self-management by employees and produce greater job satisfaction because of more worker involvement.
- People with different knowledge and skills work closely together on each team. This will broaden the knowledge and skills of each individual.

  In ABC's business process teams, graphic designers will acquire new knowledge about sales and printing. The same is true of the people with a sales and printing background. This means that all people on this team will be able to talk to customers about all aspects of the work.

- There is speedier decision making, reduced cycle times and improved responsiveness to customers.
- Because it tends to 'flatten' the organisation – that is, reduce the number of levels of management – there are reduced management costs and less need for coordination.

Drawbacks of a business process team structure

- A successful redesign to a business process structure involves a major transformation of the organisation. It is difficult, time consuming and probably very costly to make this change. New systems for virtually everything will be needed, from training, remuneration and job appraisal to inventory, accounting and management information.
- This structure works best if each process team has within it sufficient expertise and team interaction skills to handle the issues that may arise; otherwise, the company must maintain functional experts to help out as needed.

For example, the graphic design members of ABC's teams must be skilled enough to handle all the design aspects of every customer request they get.

The horizontal structure may not be suited to every organisation; however, the underlying philosophy is critical to every organisation's survival today. This is the philosophy that *everyone involved in a work process* must understand the total process, how it serves customers and how he or she contributes to it!

Team members may have a single boss, the team leader. It is also possible, however, for members to serve on a process team and still be members of a regular functional department. In this case, each member would have two bosses: the team leader and the head of the functional department. This situation is called a *matrix*, and is the fifth kind of structure we discuss.

Matrix structure

A matrix structure occurs when an employee has two (or sometimes even more) bosses in the organisation. It often accompanies the use of teams, such as project teams and business process teams. It is used when the organisation wants both to gain the benefits of teams and maintain the technical expertise of functional departments.

One example is an engineering and construction company with departments representing the functional disciplines of civil, electrical and mechanical engineering. Teams are formed to carry out specific projects; each team typically has some civil, some electrical and some mechanical engineers reporting to a project leader. But all these engineers would also report to their functional managers: the chief civil engineer, chief electrical engineer or chief mechanical engineer.

Over the course of a year, individual engineers might work for multiple project managers in addition to doing work directly for their chief engineer.

Note that in Figure 2.5 the project manager has a mechanical, a civil and an electrical engineer reporting to him. Those engineers also report to the chief mechanical engineer, chief civil engineer and chief electrical engineer, respectively. The chiefs also have some engineers on their staffs who are not matrixed to the project manager. The contract engineer is not matrixed either; the project manager is his or her only boss. (At the end of the project, the contract may be dismissed.)

Also, in this example, both the project manager and the engineering chiefs share authority over the matrixed engineers and have a major say in their promotions, rises and work.

Strengths of a matrix structure

- It enables the organisation to use its resources (people, money, facilities) efficiently because resources are moved around as projects come and go. It provides the flexibility to assign staff according to project requirements and to reassign them quickly as project requirements change.
- This structure enables the organisation to make full use of teams, and the advantages they possess, while maintaining in-depth technical expertise in critical functions.
- It gives individuals a chance to work with other employees with different skills and expertise, while still maintaining their own technical expertise (through their home department).
- It requires managers to cooperate with one another and moderates their power over their subordinates.

Drawbacks of a matrix structure

- In some cases, a matrix gets out of hand: employees end up with multiple − not just two − bosses and the resulting confusion slows down decision making.

    For example, until recently, Royal Dutch Shell had a matrix structure where some executives reported to a country, a regional and a function head. These multiple relationships slowed down decision making and cost the company money. The company has

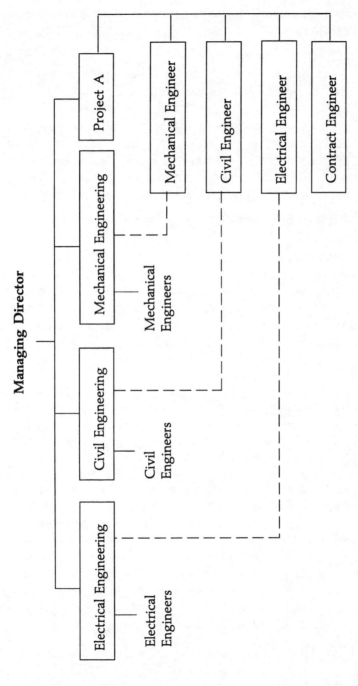

Figure 2.5 *Matrix structure in an engineering company*

now eliminated the matrix and established a more centralised operation.

- Having two or more bosses means an employee might have conflicting demands made on his or her time, and this can lead to personal stress and reduced work quality.
- Because resources are flexibly allocated in a matrix organisation, and each manager's resources go up and down according to the work coming in, there are often power struggles between managers. These can disrupt the work and get in the way of good customer service.
- Subordinates might play one boss off against the other.

Engineer Bob Smith tells the project manager, 'I'm sorry, I can't finish those calculations you needed today because my engineering chief needs me to work full-time on our departmental budget this week.' But Bob Smith has omitted to say that his chief doesn't know he has promised work for the project manager – and could get someone else to work on the budget. Bob would rather work on the budget himself and so is manipulating the situation to make it seem there is no choice.

Making a matrix work

To make a matrix work for you, make sure each participant's role, responsibilities and authority are clearly defined, preferably in writing. At the same time, reward employees for being flexible and willing to 'bend' for the good of the organisation.

In the engineering company example, a certain mechanical engineer is assigned 75 per cent of time to a project manager and 25 per cent of time to the mechanical engineering department. However (and this is a common scenario), part-way through, the project runs into unexpected difficulties and this engineer is needed full-time to help out. If the chief agrees to this reassignment, the department's work will fall behind. But the chief's work is not as high priority as the project, so the reassignment of this engineer is to the benefit of the company.

Be especially clear about performance evaluations for the

matrixed employees. People naturally tend to pay more attention to the person who will be evaluating them and determining promotions and rises. Make sure that everyone for whom an employee produces work (and this could include customers) gives input to that employee's performance evaluation.

Hybrid organisations: mixing and matching structures

When all is said and done, most larger organisations – and a lot of smaller ones too – are hybrids. That is, within each of them there is a mixture of structural forms.

For example, a giant road vehicle corporation like Ford, which has plants worldwide, will have a corporate organisation chart, subsections of which show the divisions: departments (manufacturing, marketing and sales, etc), vehicle (small/medium, light truck, etc) with smaller divisions falling under these (product strategy, design, etc).

Points to ponder

Think of two or three organisations that you know fairly well and how each one is structured.

1. If they have hybrid structures, what are they, and why do you think they were chosen?
2. What might be the consequences of choosing a different way of structuring (for example, blending functional departments into product-based departments)?

Guidelines for creating an organisation structure

Who should be involved?

The first question to answer is, 'Who should be involved?' The extent to which employees are involved in creating a structure varies. Sometimes the boss works it all out alone or every

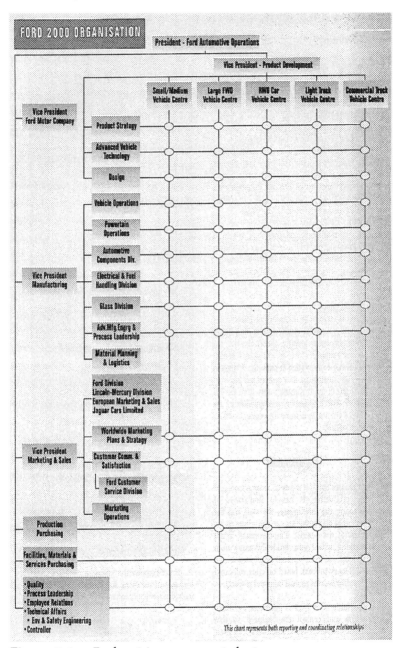

Figure 2.6. *Ford matrix management chart*
Source: Ford Motor Co Ltd

employee in the organisation might participate. And there might be any degree of involvement in between these two extremes. Some points to consider in deciding what makes sense in your situation are these:

- The more involvement people have in creating something, the more committed they will be to making it work.
- For their ideas to make sense and help the organisation to thrive, the involved employees must be both knowledgeable about the organisation's business situation and committed to its success.
- Involvement takes time. If a decision to change the organisation has to be made in a hurry, you may have to choose a less democratic process. (You don't seek consensus before moving people out of a burning building!)

Whoever is involved, it is essential that each person understands his or her role in the design project. For instance, are participants expected to:

- Give input only?
- Make recommendations to management?
- Comment on management proposals?
- Actually make design decisions?

Make sure that all boundaries and limitations are made clear at the start. For example, sometimes management knows at the outset that they will not approve any new design that increases costs or increases workforce size. It is essential the design team members know this before they start proposing design alternatives.

Whether the design is the primary responsibility of the manager in charge or of an employee design team, the basic questions to ask and steps to take are the same.

Worksheet

Start by answering the questions below. Your answers will help to point out what's working well and what can be improved with your current structure.

Questions to ask

1. How is your organisation structured now? (Draw a chart.)

2. What are the strengths and drawbacks of this structure? (It might be useful to ask others inside and outside the organisation.)

_____

_____

_____

3. How does your current structure serve or fail to serve the needs of your customers? (Ask them.)

_____

_____

_____

4. How are your business processes helped or hindered by your current structure? (Think about coordination needs – for example, which steps in each business process are highly interdependent?)

_____

_____

_____

5. **How do your employees feel about the current structure?** (Ask them if a different structure might improve their morale, productivity, opportunities for creativity?)

_____

_____

_____

6. **How might a different structure eliminate or improve weaknesses in the current one?**

_____

_____

_____

Steps in the design process
The following steps apply whether you're designing a brand-new organisation or trying to improve an existing one.

A. **Decide what's most important to you, in order of priority.** (Think back to key success factors, goals and business processes discussed in Chapter 1. Which of these might be affected by your structure?)

_____

_____

_____

B. **Draw up several alternative structures.** (On paper, draw up two or more alternative ways to structure your organisation. It helps to have employee participation at this point. It's all right to be playful at first, and essential to keep an open mind.)

C. **Evaluate each alternative in terms of advantages and drawbacks.** Judge each alternative structure according to the prioritised factors you decided on in step A above. One alternative may clearly be the winner. Or you may wish to combine features of more than one to get a structure that is right for you. Narrow the alternatives down to no more than two or three.

_____

_____

_____

D. **Prepare an organisation chart to show your preferred alternative(s).** (On paper, draw your preferred alternatives. In addition, it's a good idea to list the main functions and responsibilities for each of the 'boxes'.)

E. **Get feedback from others.** You will need feedback from those who will have to make the new structure work (managers, employees) and others who will or may be affected by it, for example, unions, customers, suppliers.

F. **Revise and finalise the structure.** Review the information you get from step E. This will help you to choose one plan if you had more than one resulting from step C. It will also undoubtedly lead to some fine-tuning of the final choice.

If you would really like to try something new, but are not sure it will work:

- Do it anyway if it's a _small change_. Keep an eye on it, and be prepared to modify or reverse your decision if things don't work out.
- Consider having a pilot test if it's a _big change_. Set up the pilot for a specified period, and have 'before' and 'after' measures of the factors that are critical to your organisation's success. Be fully prepared to make major adjustments to your proposed new structure if things don't work out. Do not pressurise people to make the pilot succeed at any price!

You have just completed one important part of designing an organisation – deciding how to divide up the work. It is now time to consider the next major piece of organisation design – the management structure.

Asking for feedback on a proposed new structure

Whether or not you involve others in creating a new organisation structure, it is very important that you get their ideas on what you propose to do *before you try to implement it.*

Prepare an organisation chart that lists the major functions of each department shown. Get input from the people who have to make it work and the people who will be most affected by it. Consider:

- Customers
- Employees
- Other departments (if part of a larger company)
- Unions
- Suppliers
- Community groups
- Regulators (if a regulated company).

Ask questions such as the following:

- What do you like about this proposed organisation structure?
- What things do you think would work better if we changed to this?
- What do you not like about it? Why not?
- What changes can you suggest that would make it work better?
- What would we need to do to make sure this gets implemented smoothly?

More specifically, what would be the likely impact of these suggested changes on:

- Getting important work done?
- Coordinating tasks in a business process?
- Staffing levels?
- Rewards and benefits?
- Need for training?
- Bargaining unit agreements?
- Work space, facilities and equipment?
- Information systems?
- Communications – inside and outside the company?
- Costs of production?
- Community relations?
- Any other important factors in your organisation?

CHAPTER 3
Management Structure

Management structure consists of three main factors: the *hierarchy* or number of management levels, the *span of control* and how *centralised* or *decentralised* decision making in the organisation is. First, some definitions.

- *Management hierarchy* refers to the number of levels of management and supervision. A *flat* structure is one with few levels; a *tall* structure has many levels.
- *Span of control* refers to the number of people who report to one manager or supervisor. If there are very few people, we call this a *narrow* span of control; if there are many people, we call it a *broad* span of control.
- An organisation is *centralised* to the extent that major decisions, control over resources and authority to take action are in the hands of only a few top people; it is *decentralised* to the extent people at lower levels are able to make decisions, control resources and take action in their part of the organisation.

These factors are closely linked. For instance, any time a company adds a level of management, assuming it does not add to its total number of employees, its average span of control will become narrower. Figure 3.1 illustrates how span of control changes when an organisation moves from two to three to four levels. Of course, the reverse is also true.

Total number of people in each example = 12

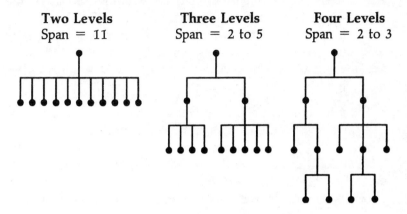

Figure 3.1. *Spans of control and levels of management*

Management hierarchy

All people who draw a pay cheque from an organisation are *employees*. *Managers* are those people who are responsible for directing, coordinating and controlling the work of others. It is common to refer to the people who report to a manager as *subordinates*; however, this term may have a connotation of inferiority, and throughout this book we generally use the word *workers*, rather than subordinates, to refer to non-managerial employees.

There are three levels of management. Top-level managers are those occupying the highest positions in the organisation. A small company may have only one top-level manager: the proprietor or managing director. The larger the company, the more top-level managers there will be; they will generally be the people who report directly to the managing director.

First-level managers are those who directly supervise workers. In a big organisation, this is the lowest level of management. Middle- managers are those occupying management levels between the top level and the first level. Large companies often have several levels of middle management. Today, increasing numbers of business firms are re-examining the need for some of their middle- management positions, which are prime targets for elimination in efforts to 'flatten' the organisation (as we describe later).

All these levels form what is called a *hierarchy* or *chain of command*. Power, authority and influence typically – although not always, as we shall see – raise a person's position in this hierarchy.

- *Power* in an organisation is defined as the ability to control the actions and decisions of others even if they resist. A person who holds a high position in an organisation has power by virtue of that position; this is called *positional power*.
- *Authority* refers to the right to make decisions – about what others should do and how they do it, how much money to spend on what, and so on. Authority is formally granted by the organisation; it is thus *legitimate power*.
- *Influence* is the ability to affect what others do or believe, regardless of whether or not one has the authority to do so,
- *Accountability* refers to the state of being held answerable for results.

Exceptions to the rule

We said earlier that there are exceptions to the general rule that the higher up the hierarchy a person is, the greater that person's power, influence and authority. Exceptions occur:

- When people at lower levels have special knowledge, skills or external connections not shared by those at higher levels and these are critical to that organisation's success.

  For example: technical experts in non-managerial positions in high technology companies often exert considerable influence on the company's decisions; sometimes their salaries are greater than those of employees at higher levels.

- When a lower-level person is in a position that allows him or her to control access to higher-level positions.

  Frequently, a high-level executive's secretary has the power, though not the authority, to control who has access to the executive. This person may have influence too if the boss has confidence in her or his judgement.

● When authority is delegated to lower levels. In some cases, people who have the authority to make certain kinds of decision may delegate that authority to people at lower levels. Typically, in these cases, both the person delegating and the person delegated to will share accountability for results.

For example, a department manager may have the authority to hire and fire all employees in that department. He may delegate this authority to the first-level supervisors who report to him, because he feels they are better able to judge the qualifications and performance of their workers. With formal delegation of this authority, the first-line supervisors do not have to get the manager's approval any time they hire or fire someone. But both manager and supervisors are jointly accountable for the overall level and quality of staffing in the department.

Flat and tall hierarchies
It obviously makes a big difference to the individual where in the hierarchy he or she is placed. It also makes a big difference to the organisation how many management levels it has. Every management level added to or removed from the organisation affects how work is done, the way employees feel about their work and the cost of management.

Adding a level
An example will help to illustrate what typically happens when a company adds an extra level of management.

When Bill Beaumont started his machine shop, Beaumont Machining, he had three employees: one to handle the office work and two machinists. Then his business expanded, and he hired two more machinists. With more of his time spent in managing the overall business, he had less time for resolving the day-to-day issues that arose in the machine shop. So Bill appointed his senior machinist, Mike, to be supervisor over the other three machinists.

Thus Beaumont Machining moved from a two-level organisation to a three-level one, at least in the machine shop (see Figure 3.2). Note that this is still a two-level organisation as far as the office administrator position is concerned.

As two-level structure

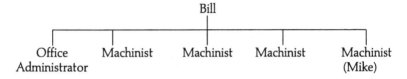

As three-level structure

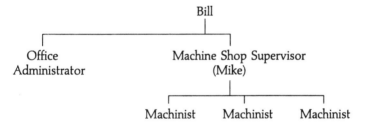

Figure 3.2. *Beaumont Machining*

Consider what impact this additional level of organisation has on Bill, Mike and the three machinists.

- *Bill is now freed from having to manage the day-to-day issues that arise in running the machines; he thus has a lot more time available to spend on getting new business, working with customers and managing company finances.*
- *Mike now has a chance to acquire supervisory skills and make many more decisions than he did previously. As he becomes adept at handling personnel issues, work scheduling and quality control, he will even further relieve the load on Bill.*
- *The three machinists find Mike much more available to answer questions and help resolve problems than Bill was, given Bill's*

much broader range of responsibilities. On the other hand, they are now one step removed from the 'boss'. Suggestions and concerns they have must first be referred to Mike who may then need to consult Bill.

- *Mike, in his position as go-between, has the opportunity to slow down or speed up, clarify or distort communication between Bill and the machinists, and vice versa. Mike can ease Bill's load by reducing the amount of information that Bill receives; however, problems may arise if Bill gets too far out of touch with issues in the machine shop.*

Removing a level

Here's an example of what happens when a company removes a level of management.

Personnel Services International (PSI) provides human resources services to corporations throughout Europe and North America. Until recently, it had a head office in the United States, 17 regional offices (14 in North America and three in Europe), and local offices in all major metropolitan areas on both continents.

While its business has been growing steadily, its profit margins have been getting smaller and its competition fiercer. After a major corporate review of cost-cutting opportunities, PSI decided to eliminate its regional offices. Some employees have been reassigned to local offices or to corporate headquarters, but many have been discharged.

Thus, PSI moved from a three-level company to a two-level one. Consider the impact of the removal of the regional level on the local offices as well as on employees at corporate headquarters.

- *Managers of the local offices and their employees have more autonomy and responsibility — to generate and fulfil new business contracts, to keep track of financial and accounting information, to staff and manage projects and to ensure customer satisfaction in all areas.*
- *The support that people in the local offices used to get from the*

regional staff is no longer available; some support is available from headquarters, but there are fewer people there so it often takes longer to get help.

- *The systems developers at headquarters interact more with the local offices; this means they get a lot of information useful to development efforts about what works and what doesn't in different situations.*
- *Corporate finance and accounting staff have to manage and reconcile all the information coming in from local offices. There are no regional staff to help them with this.*

We have used one small company and one fairly large company as examples, but note that the effects are similar no matter how large or small the organisation. In fact, we can make the following statements about flat and tall organisation structures.

In a flat organisation – that is, one with relatively few management levels:

- Communication throughout the organisation is generally faster and less distorted.
- Decisions can be made more quickly, which means that the company can be faster in responding to customers.
- Employees at lower levels feel more in touch with top management.
- The support that could be provided by more levels of management must be obtained by other means: by having more self-sufficient employees at the lower levels or in the way work is done.
- On the downside, there are fewer opportunities for promotion as there are fewer levels to move up to.

In a tall organisation – that is, one with relatively numerous levels:

- Because the average span of control is narrower, the supervisory load is less for each manager. Tighter supervision may in some cases result in more productive work units – for example, when low productivity and poor quality of results appear to result from workers not understanding or not following procedures.

- There are more opportunities for promotion because there are more 'steps in the ladder' for people to climb.
- Communication is slower and likely to be less accurate. This is because:
  1. *The more links there are in a communication chain, the greater the likelihood of distortion.*
  2. *People tend to communicate more easily with others at the same organisational level.*
- Decisions take longer to make. This is especially true where there is a tall functional management structure that requires coordination across the functional boundaries.

Points to ponder

As we have seen, broad spans and flat hierarchies have drawbacks as well as advantages. How might you go about improving the major drawbacks of a flat organisation? For example:

1. What incentives could you provide to people at lower levels in the organisation to make up for there not being many opportunities for promotion 'up the ladder'?
2. How can you prevent 'overspanned' managers becoming overwhelmed by supervisory duties?
3. How can you help new or relatively unskilled employees in a flat organisation to get the support their overspanned boss is too busy to provide?
4. How can you organise work so that less supervision is needed to accomplish the same results?

Organisation size and structure

Size is one of the most important variables affecting an organisation's structure. As they grow, most organisations follow a similar evolutionary pattern, as illustrated in Table 3.1.

When an organisation starts out as a one-person enterprise (stage 1 in the table), that person performs all the tasks he or

Table 3.1.	Evolution of a hypothetical organisation as size increases		
	Company size	No of levels	Division of work
Stage 1: Single owner	1	1	None – one person does it all
Stage 2: Takes on four employees	5	2	Individuals perform specialised functions
Stage 3: Departments formed. First-level supervisors recruited	50	3	Functional departments
Stage 4: Middle management level created	500	4	Functional departments
Stage 5: Multiple levels of middle management	5000	4–8	Functional or product/ customer focused
Stage 6: Functional organisation becomes unwieldy	50,000	6–12	Product/customer-focused divisions
Stage 7: Company tries to recapture benefits of 'smallness'	65,000	'Flattens' 4–6	Divisions as profit centres and autonomous operations

she is capable of, and contracts out the rest to external providers. For example, if this is a manufacturing business, the owner/proprietor may handle sales, design and manufacture of the product, delivery and invoicing. He or she may contract out secretarial and bookkeeping services, cleaning, maintenance and legal services.

As the company grows (stage 2), the owner will take on some employees, and these people will probably specialise in certain functions. So a division of labour appears. For example, the owner may recruit a sales representative, a product designer and a machinist to make the product. The owner may also hire an office administrator to handle secretarial and bookkeeping work and thus reduce the amount of work contracted out.

At stage 3, the company gets even bigger, we will find departments rather than individuals to handle functions so another level of management is added: a sales manager to handle a group of sales representatives, a design manager to manage a group of designers, and so on.

As the organisation gets bigger still (stage 4), middle levels of management appear. Now the sales department may be split up into several sections according to the territory served: each section will have a first-line supervisor managing it, first-line supervisors will report to the sales manager, who reports to the managing director.

Initially, most organisations start by being functionally organised. When they become large (stage 5), they often split into divisions that are organised by product, customer or geographical area served. These divisions often have functional departments within each.

By the time an organisation grows extremely large (stage 6), it commonly spends more time and resources on maintaining itself than on serving its customers. Today, when being attentive to and responding quickly to changing markets is critical to survival, these top-heavy companies find that their size inhibits their ability to compete successfully. A large organisation is very slow to change, even when its managers understand the need to do so.

Large companies try in different ways to capture the speed and flexibility of smaller companies (stage 7). Sometimes they split into comparatively independent divisions – becoming, in effect, a cluster of 'little companies'.

For example, some years ago, Hewlett Packard Corporation found that its growing size was hindering its ability to succeed in the highly competitive scientific instrument and small-computer market. The company split up into small, relatively autonomous divisions that were able to generate their own resources and make their own business decisions. It became a company policy to keep division size to about 1000 employees; if a division gets significantly larger than this, the company considers spinning off a separate unit.

Some companies shed all functions that are not a part of their core business – for example, support functions such as secretarial services, reprographic services, payroll and other human resource systems. Instead of performing these functions in house, they contract with external suppliers, rather as a smaller company would.

Other companies restructure into teams that have enough autonomy to enable them to respond to customers' concerns quickly and effectively.

Span of control

The question of what is a proper span of control has been much debated. A ratio of five workers to one supervisor was proposed by the 'scientific management' theorists of the 1930s and until recent times a span of five to seven has been seen as ideal. In the last ten years or so, however, this supposed ideal has been challenged as being far too narrow. The emphasis today is on broadening spans of control so as to flatten organisations.

Before we go further, let's see what difference it makes to have a relatively narrow or broad span of control.

With a narrow span of control:

- Cost of management is greater, simply because there are more managers for a given number of workers.
- Everything else being equal, with fewer workers to supervise, each manager has more time and energy for managerial duties and for non-managerial work.
- With closer supervision, workers get more individual attention and support from the boss, but also have less autonomy and less opportunity for self-direction.
- There are likely to be more levels of hierarchy with the accompanying features of a tall structure – such as slower communication and more difficulty coordinating among work groups.

With a broad span of control:

- Costs of management are lower.

- The supervisory task is more difficult, because managers have to spread their efforts among more workers. This means that other ways must be found to handle coordination, communication and other work that the company relies on managers to do.
- Workers are encouraged to develop skill and initiative; they have more opportunity to exercise their own judgement in making decisions about their work. This is a major source of job satisfaction for many people.
- To the extent that broader spans result in fewer organisation levels, there is more direct communication between people at the lowest and highest levels of the organisation.
- On the downside, workers who need or want close support from the boss are less likely to get it.

You can see that the nature of the work as well as the skill and experience of non-managerial employees come into play in deciding span of control. Another point to consider is that many 'working supervisors' have considerable responsibility apart from supervision. For example, a sales manager might directly handle a number of customer accounts and have only a small amount of time to supervise other sales personnel. For these people, a narrow span of control might be quite appropriate.

Centralisation and decentralisation

We now come to the important issue of who makes what kind of decisions and controls what kind of resources. As we said earlier, when we talk about organisations as centralised or decentralised we are referring to how concentrated or dispersed is the authority to make decisions. Today, most organisation experts say decisions should be made as far down in the organisation and as close to the customer as possible, making for maximum responsiveness to customer needs. This implies decentralisation. Many of today's successful companies take this philosophy to heart.

For example, Hewlett Packard in the 1980s had 38 central committees that ruled most major aspects of its business. This structure slowed down the company's ability to react to changes in its competitive environment. Recognising this, in 1990 the company dissolved these committees and decentralised most of the authority to the divisions.

In spite of this, as you will read time and again in today's business press, other large companies appear to be doing the opposite: they are centralising functions that were formerly decentralised. In fact, organisations commonly swing from centralised to decentralised and back again as their circumstances change and priorities alter.

Three major reasons to centralise

Control
Centralisation is an organisation's most reliable method of controlling and coordinating activity and resources. Central control is especially important:

- When the company as a whole has to meet legal or regulatory requirements that are difficult to interpret
- When decisions made at a local level will affect the whole company – for example, a local division's interpretation of the company's contract with a union will be binding on the whole company
- When what occurs in one part of the company will affect every other part – as would be the case with a company-wide system or network like the transmission system in a utility company.

Cost
Because of economies of scale, a centralised function can generally be managed with fewer resources than a decentralised function.

Consider the purchasing function in a large company. With purchasing for the whole company done in a central department, the company can get better quantity discounts than would be available to any single division. Any time a large number of similar tasks are performed in one place, economies are possible because equipment and facilities can be shared, and generally fewer people are needed to do the work.

New technology
Over recent decades, the rate of technological change has been phenomenal. New technology enables many a decentralised company to centralise, and vice versa.

Three major reasons to decentralise

Responsiveness
With decision making pushed down to a local level, the company can respond more quickly to customers and local conditions.

Independence
Decentralisation tends to stimulate creativity and independence in people at lower levels and helps to build a pool of candidates for higher-level positions.

New technology
New computer technology enables companies to decentralise authority to a much greater extent than was previously possible. One of the main reasons for centralising authority is to ensure that top management knows about and can influence what is happening throughout the organisation. Today's sophisticated information systems enable authority to be delegated downwards while still keeping top management well informed.

Factors to consider in centralising or decentralising
Here is a good rule of thumb to follow.

Make sure decisions are made by people who are as close as possible to the source of information and the field of action; this way, you will get quicker and better informed decisions. Yet recognise that some decisions may have to be centralised for the good of the total organisation.

In some large organisations, there is a formal *delegation of authority* system, which specifies who makes what decisions. This is an issue that needs to be considered carefully. Some factors to take into account in delegating authority include:

- *Duration*
  How far into the future does the decision commit the organisation? How fast can it be reversed?

  Generally speaking, the more long term the decision and the more difficult it is to reverse, the more senior the decision makers need to be.

- *Impact*
  What is the effect of the decision on other departments or divisions or on the organisation as a whole?

  The more the decision affects the organisation as a whole or other parts of the organisation, the more senior the decision makers need to be involved.

- *Cost*
  What is the cost of implementing the decision? You need to take into account not only the cost of resources — such as people, money, materials — but also more subtle factors such as possible loss of customer confidence or employee morale. What would it cost to reverse the decision and its consequences?

  The higher the cost, the more senior-level decision makers will be involved.

Points to ponder

Both centralisation and decentralisation have some advantages and drawbacks.

1. If you wanted to centralise some functions in order to cut costs, how might you use technology to retain responsiveness to customers?
2. In what other ways could a mainly centralised company make sure it is responsive to customers at a local level?

Putting it all together

As you can see, the three factors of span of control, levels of hierarchy and centralisation or decentralisation of decisions are often interrelated. Narrow spans tend to accompany tall structures and centralised decision making. Broad spans tend to go with flat structures and decentralised decision making. These broad generalisations apply much of the time, but there are exceptions.

Guidelines for creating management structure

Perhaps the most important piece of advice we can offer is, don't let it 'just happen'. All too often management structure is not the result of careful thought and planning, but rather a consequence of other changes. For example, changes in workforce size — up or down — often leave managers with much broader or narrower spans of control than they had before.

Or, as in the Beaumont Machining example given earlier, a top manager appoints a middle manager to relieve the load on the top, and this has the 'ripple effects' of an extra level. These include changing people's work responsibilities, communication patterns and what sorts of decisions they make.

In reviewing your management structure, think about the intended and unintended consequences of the number of levels of hierarchy, the spans of control and the levels at which decisions are made. These can affect your goals, key success factors and business processes.

Who should be involved?

People at higher levels
A level of management is typically added or eliminated as a result of a decision made by the level above it. This is because some strain felt by the higher-level managers is creating the perceived need for change.

At Beaumont Machining, the higher-level person (Bill Beaumont) experienced work overload that was relieved by creating a supervisory level in the machine shop. In the case of PSI, top management wanted to cut costs, and eliminating the regional level was one way to do this.

People at lower levels who are affected
Whoever makes the decision, it is valuable to get input from everyone who would be directly affected by such a move.

In the Beaumont Machining case, Bill Beaumont met Mike first to get his reactions to the proposal to make him a supervisor over the other machinists. Then, he and Mike held a meeting of all machinists. Mike's new role was explained and the machinists were asked for their questions and reactions. As a result, many issues about people's responsibilities were clarified. It was explained under what circumstances a machinist could approach Bill directly rather than going through Mike. By having this discussion beforehand, the new structure worked smoothly from the start.

Others inside or outside the company
Creating or removing a level of management is likely to affect relationships with other departments inside the company and with customers and suppliers outside. You may not wish to involve these people in the decision to add or remove a level, but it is important to communicate the change to anyone whose business relationship would be affected, answer their questions and address their concerns.

Ways to gather information
It may be difficult for a manager or a design team by themselves to answer the questions on the worksheet. Some ways to gather information are by:

Observing. See what is happening in terms of results.

Asking people. Get the views of people at different levels of the organisation and, if appropriate, people outside the organisation such as customers and suppliers.

Experimenting. For example, when a supervisory position is vacant, the manager might try having subordinates report directly to the former supervisor's boss and then ask questions about what worked well and what didn't.

Benchmarking. Find out what other companies do in similar circumstances.

Reading and research. What have the experiences of others been in your own or related industries?

Remember. It is essential that decisions on management structure benefit the company in terms of your key success factors and serving your business processes. Think especially about customer satisfaction, product timeliness and quality, costs of production and company profitability, employee satisfaction and development.

Worksheet

Answering the following questions for each part of the organisation you're designing will help you to think through your own situation.

Levels of hierarchy

1. **How many levels of management do you have in your present or proposed organisation?** (Remember, the number of levels might be different in different parts of your organisation.)

_____

_____

2. **What the costs and benefits to the company as a whole of having each level of management?** To each manager or supervisor? To the workers reporting to each manager?

_____

_____

3. **Thinking in terms of your goals, business processes and key success factors, are there places where it might be desirable to eliminate a level of management?** What would be the possible drawbacks or benefits of doing this? How would the work formerly done by the managers at that level be handled?

_____

_____

_____

4. **Are there places where it might be beneficial to add a level of management?** What value would it contribute to the organisation? What might be the disadvantages of doing this, and can they be overcome?

_____

_____

_____

Spans of control

5. **What is the span of control for each of the managers and supervisors in your organisation?**

_____

_____

_____

6. **Do any of these seem to warrant investigation?** (Suggestion: look first at spans of four or under and spans of ten or more.)

_____

_____

_____

7. Describe any problems you have noted that might be due to too narrow or too broad a span.

   _____

   _____

   _____

8. **Might it make sense to consider changing the span of control in particular cases?** What do the managers and supervisors involved think?

   _____

   _____

   _____

9. **Will changing spans of control lead to more or fewer levels of hierarchy?** If so, what would be the 'ripple effects' of this?

   _____

   _____

   _____

10. **If you're broadening spans of control, what are your plans to change the expectations and skills of managers and workers so they can work successfully with the new span?** What else needs to change to make the new span work?

    _____

    _____

    _____

Decision making

11. What kinds of decision can be made and actions

taken at each level in your organisation?

_____

_____

_____

12. Are there some decisions that could be delegated to lower levels?

_____

_____

_____

13. What would be the consequences of doing this in specific cases in terms of your goals, business processes and success factors?

_____

_____

_____

14. What additional knowledge and skills will be needed for employees at lower levels to make these decisions? How would people's roles and jobs change?

_____

_____

_____

15. What decisions *must* be centralised at the top level of the organisation, and why?

_____

_____

_____

CHAPTER 4
Coordination and Control

Once structures are in place for dividing up and managing the work, you need techniques for ensuring that activities are coordinated and the right work gets done in the right way.

This chapter describes four techniques for coordinating and controlling work: supervision; standardisation; building employee commitment; and teams. It also includes guidelines for selecting your own techniques.

The whole point of creating structure is to divide work into manageable units and make it clear who is responsible for what. You now need to decide on techniques for:

1. *Coordinating* the work: integrating the activities of different people working to produce the same end product or service.
2. *Controlling* the work: making sure people are doing what they need to be doing and are doing it in the right way.
3. *Measuring* performance: finding out to what extent you are reaching your goals and targets.

This chapter describes techniques for coordinating and controlling work, and presents guidelines for selecting your own techniques. Performance measurement is covered in Chapter 5.

Coordination and control techniques

In practice, the two activities of coordinating and controlling overlap; the very act of coordinating implies that some control is occurring. For this reason, we discuss them together. However, it is possible to coordinate using one technique and to control using another, as we'll discuss.

There are four basic techniques that organisations use to make sure that work is coordinated and controlled. Commonly, you'll find all methods used within the same company. different companies, or different departments within the same company, may lean towards one method to coordinate work and another to control work. The four techniques are:

1. Supervision
2. Standardisation
3. Building employee commitment
4. Teams.

1. Supervision

A supervisor coordinates by establishing priorities and schedules, assigning people to tasks, making sure that interdependent activities are correctly timed. In addition to integrating the work efforts of people within the unit, the supervisor also helps to link the work of the whole unit to other units in the company.

A supervisor exercises control (a) through monitoring workers' behaviour − for example, watching and directing them as they work, and/or (b) by examining finished work and instructing workers to make corrections if warranted.

It is possible to use supervision to coordinate but not control work, as the following example shows:

At Beaumont Machining, the new supervisor, Mike, carries out many traditional supervisory tasks such as assigning work and preparing work schedules. However, each machinist is fully trained and typically completes each assignment without needing to consult him. Control over each machinist's work occurs through the use of standard operating procedures and specifications set for the final product. (See the discussion of standardisation of process and outcomes later in this chapter.) In other words, Beaumont uses Mike primarily to coordinate rather than control work.

Contrast the above case with the situation of telephone operators whose supervisors both coordinate and control their work.

Telephone operators are arranged at computer consoles in a room with a supervisor observing them, keeping track of the amount of time each is spending per call, and sometimes listening in to monitor conversations. Information operators are expected to take an average of no more than six seconds per call. If an operator needs to take a break, he or she must signal the supervisor and get permission before leaving the station.

This is an example of supervision used to control performance. Supervisors watch what the workers are doing and how they're doing it and give immediate feedback on performance. These supervisors also coordinate work by planning schedules, arranging for replacements to take the place of absent workers, and so on.

Supervision and spans of control
The shape of the management structure we discussed in the last chapter has an effect on the extent to which supervision is a feasible means of control. In cases where the structure is flat and spans of control are broad, supervisors may still coordinate activities, but the company must use other methods to control what work is done and how. Where the structure is tall and spans are narrow, supervision is feasible for both control and coordination.

When to use supervision
Besides span of control, there are several other factors that affect how appropriate it is to use supervision as a primary coordination and/or control method. In general, supervision is a good option to consider when:

- Interdependence among the positions supervised is high.
- The supervisor has special knowledge about the work that workers do not share.
- Timing is critical and having close supervision is the best way to ensure it.
- Errors could be costly — for example, when the work is dangerous.
- The work is complex and unpredictable, and workers lack the knowledge, experience or motivation to make decisions about the exceptions to routine that arise.

Potential drawbacks of using supervision to control
Whether or not your situation warrants using supervision to control work, there are some potential negative consequences.

- Employees' creativity and initiative may be stifled, especially if the supervisor tends to monitor their actions closely.
- Workers may learn to deny personal responsibility for their work and instead rely on the supervisor to catch mistakes.
- Employees may put more effort into keeping their supervisor happy than in trying to satisfy the customer.
- If the supervisor's expertise and experience are no greater than those of the employees, he/she may not have credibility when trying to monitor and correct their work.

2. Standardisation
The second major technique used to coordinate and control is standardisation. This means setting standards and criteria to make sure that events follow a predictable path and produce predictable outcomes. It is possible to standardise:

- *Work process*, or how things are done
- *Outcomes* of the work, such as products and services
- *Inputs* to the work, such as the credentials of employees and the quality of materials and equipment.

Standardising process
Standardising process simply means having rules, procedures or policies that specify how things are to be done.

The assembly line, as originally conceived, is a perfect example of an attempt to standardise a work process. Often, the 'what, when, and how' of every step in the assembly process was specified in detail down to the number of hand and arm movements and footsteps to take.

Nearly all organisations standardise some processes to some degree, but seldom to the extent of the assembly line described. In fact, today even assembly lines are not so rigid; workers typically have more discretion in terms of rotating tasks and taking action to ensure quality – sometimes even stopping the line if they think it necessary.

Process rules might be communicated verbally and informally. The new order clerk is told: 'Every time you get an order for A-type widgets, give it to Joe. Give orders for B-type widgets to Sally.'

Or there might be hefty policy manuals and standard operating procedures that spell out every step of every work process. In some cases, employees are sent to training classes to learn how to do their jobs. Many trades have long apprenticeship periods before workers are considered sufficiently skilled to function as journeymen.

When to use standardisation of work processes
Standardisation of work processes may be *useful*:

- If the work is routine, with few exceptions to the rules
- If demands for the product or service are predictable
- As an alternative to supervision when the span of control is broad
- If workers' activities are visible and measurable.

Standardisation of work processes may be *essential* when:

- The customer or an external agency has specified procedures that must be followed (as is often the case in military or other government contracts); and/or
- The way things are done is critical to how they come out.

  For example, in constructing a new building, each step from foundation to roof has to follow procedures to meet building regulations. Furthermore, if the cement for the foundation is not mixed in the right way, laid in the right way and allowed to set for the right time, the resulting foundation may not have the strength to hold the building.

Potential drawbacks of standardising work process
- Many people find it boring and demoralising to have no control over how they do their work. They may withdraw their attention and lose enthusiasm, and work quality and productivity may suffer.
- Employees who are instructed to follow detailed process steps are less likely to think of ways to improve the process – and over time there is room for improvement in almost every process.
- It is also entirely possible to 'standardise' error or waste into a process, leading to inferior quality and inefficiency.

Points to ponder
In situations where it is essential for the entire work process to be standardised, how can you encourage workers to show initiative and be alert to opportunities for improvement?

Standardising outcomes
Standardising outcomes means specifying that final results must meet certain standards or criteria. Sometimes, companies rely on outcomes alone to coordinate and control work. Consider the following situation.

The sales representatives working for a company that makes food-loading conveyors spend most of their time in the field. To be successful in their work, they have to understand the customer's situation and recommend the most appropriate equipment; often, this equipment is tailored for the customer. They are skilled engineers as well as salespeople.

These employees cannot be supervised in person, nor is it a good idea to specify what steps they have to follow in doing their job. On the contrary, it is in the company's interests for them to be creative and flexible. Therefore, the company can best control performance by looking at the outcomes of their work: for example, the number of conveyors sold, new customers brought in, customer satisfaction ratings, or profit made for the company.

Points to ponder

The risk of controlling through outcomes alone is that poor performance isn't discovered until 'after the fact'. How can the company in the example above try to maximise the likelihood that their representatives will, indeed, get good results?

When should outcomes not be standardised?

It is always appropriate — in fact, it is essential — to make clear what results are expected from work activity. All companies have, or should have, goals to be met. However, it's not always desirable to be too specific about what kind of results you're holding employees to. This would be the case when the outcome itself is not clear — for example, when developing a new product or trying to break new ground.

A software engineer in an entertainment software company has the task of developing a new computer game. The development group is virtually 'cut loose' in order to work on this. Results expected are stated very broadly: it must be a game that customers will buy and that can be produced at a profit. Being bright and creative people, members of the design team are more likely to benefit the company by being given the freedom to experiment, perhaps make some false starts and develop a final product whose parameters they simply didn't know when they started out.

Note that the expected results aren't left entirely open-ended. The expectation is that the product will sell and can be produced at a profit. But the company is willing to tolerate some false starts, and not to specify price, quantity, quality, target market and other criteria they might normally set in advance for finished products.

The two above examples illustrate the following general statements about standardising outcomes.

Consider standardising outcomes rather than standardising process or using supervision when:

- Span of control is too broad for supervision to be a good alternative
- Interdependence is low
- Outcomes are visible and measurable
- The supervisor is not as knowledgeable as the worker concerning how to do the work
- Workers are sufficiently experienced, skilled and dedicated to the company's success to be trusted to do the work the right way
- The organisation wishes to encourage worker initiative and creativity.

Don't be too specific about the outcomes expected when:

- Management has only a very general idea of what the final product will be so it is difficult to specify outcomes ahead of time; and
- The company can afford to use resources in an exploratory or developmental project, such as in the software company example above.

Standardising inputs
Another way that companies control work is by making sure that the resources that go into the work meet certain criteria. These resources include the knowledge and skills of people employed to work on a job, as well as tools, materials, equipment and so on.

Standardising people. There are many positions that companies fill by hiring unskilled workers. The fast food industry is a classic example. But, in other cases – and these are increasing as work becomes more complex – organisations rely heavily on recruiting employees who already have special skills and experience.

Sometimes the new employees will be the only ones in the organisation with those special skills. In these cases, it's difficult for company management to control through supervision, or by standardising processes or outcomes – at least initially. Instead, they rely heavily on the qualifications of the people they hire: academic or technical training, experience, references from former employers and so on.

Standardising materials and equipment. Companies also standardise inputs by setting standards and specifications for goods and services purchased from suppliers. In some cases, there might also be some physical inspection of the goods, especially with a new supplier or one that hasn't lived up to its commitments in the past.

One of the primary strategies of *total quality management* is to establish minimum standards for parts and require suppliers to meet these standards. The quality certification process called ISO 9000 establishes a whole set of requirements for relationships with suppliers that organisations seeking to be officially designated 'world class' must meet.

3. Building employee commitment
A third coordination and control technique is to have employees who are so dedicated to the success of the organisation that they can be relied on to do the best work possible and cooperate fully with others to make sure the desired results are achieved.

This commitment must not be blind. It must be based on an understanding of the organisation's business situation and strategies, its problems and opportunities and the way the employee can contribute to its success. Also, to be fully motivated, the individual must see some overlap between company goals and personal goals.

The idea of commitment based on shared goals and values is at the heart of the interest in corporate culture as a potential competitive advantage. Corporate culture refers to the set of beliefs, values and behaviours that characterise an organisation.

To a great extent, the realisation that corporate culture could provide competitive advantage came from studies of Hewlett-Packard. Hewlett-Packard developed a way of doing business called the 'HP Way'. The HP Way refers to the basic principles of encouraging and supporting individual creativity and initiative, freedom of action to achieve both personal and company goals, building the highest value products, treating people well and sharing the rewards of success. The HP Way provides guidelines and support to help employees contribute their best efforts even in unfamiliar situations.

It is becoming increasingly recognised that an employee's commitment to the success of the organisation is a critical success factor. Approaches such as employee involvement, continuous improvement and total quality are all based on:

- The premise that the people who do the work know the most about it and are the best source of ideas for improvement.
- The idea that commitment to the company's success is critical in helping it to beat the competition.

Commitment and the employee
As we said earlier, commitment to the organisation depends at least in part on some perceived overlap between the individual's goals and the organisation's goals. There are many other factors that characterise an organisation with a high degree of employee commitment.

Factors that increase commitment:

- *Inspiring mission and shared values.* Values are deeply held beliefs about what is good and desirable. Some employees are drawn to a company because of its mission and values.
- *Visionary leadership.* Inspiring leaders can communicate the organisation's mission and values in a way that motivates employees to follow. Visionary leaders project an image of the future that arouses energy and enthusiasm in their followers.

- *Shared glory and sacrifice.* This means employees share the rewards when things go right, and everyone, including top management, shares the sacrifice when the organisation isn't doing so well.
- *Employees are involved.* Employees at all levels are involved in setting goals, planning the work and solving problems that arise. Employee suggestions are taken seriously, and there are reasonable explanations when suggestions are turned down.
- *Employees know how they're doing.* Performance results are shared so that employees know how they personally, the unit, and the whole organisation, are doing. Good work is acknowledged and rewarded.
- *Employees understand where they fit.* Employees understand how their part of the work fits with other parts and how it links to the end product or service. Some organisational experts believe that a broad scope of work and a high degree of employee control over how it's done also contribute to a high degree of commitment.
- *Managers are good communicators.* People are more likely to be influenced by their immediate supervisor than by any other form of communication in the company. Managers and supervisors who are dedicated to the company's success have a powerful impact in shaping the attitudes of employees.

Factors that erode commitment:

- *Lack of job security.* Commitment is perceived as a two-way street. When job security is threatened, and especially if this happens often, people start to question the organisation's commitment to its employees.
- *Management incompetence.* Perceived evidence of incompetent, arbitrary or unethical behaviour in managers decreased employee trust in the organisation.
- *Management isn't 'walking the talk'.* This is the perception that others in the organisation, especially top management, are not themselves doing what they expect other employees to do.

Too much reliance on employee commitment:

- *Underorganisation.* Organisations that rely very heavily on employee commitment may pay too little attention to structure and procedures. As a result, the organisation is not as efficient or as effective as it might be.
- *Overidentification.* Employees sometimes become too identified with the organisation. Their high degree of commitment results in their becoming 'burned out' in its service.
- *Opposition is silenced.* When employees are strongly bound together in pursuit of a common cause, it's difficult for anyone to disagree with the organisation's direction and ways of doing things. Dissidents are pressured into accepting the status quo, or they may leave the organisation. This means that if change becomes necessary due to a changing business environment, the organisation is slow to react.

4. Teams

As we read and hear every day in the news media, the world of business is changing at an ever-accelerating pace. Often, traditional methods of coordinating work – such as supervision and standardisation – simply aren't enough to get the fast changes and quick results needed to survive and thrive in today's environment.

Work teams designed to fit the requirements and opportunities of particular business settings are frequently the answer. Teams are especially useful when there is a need for flexibility and speed in handling work and when it's important to have input from different parts of the organisation simultaneously.

In Chapter 2 we described a type of organisation structure that is based on business process teams. However, there are many different kinds of team and they can be found in all types of organisation: functional, product-based, customer-based and matrix.

The business process teams we described are relatively permanent in nature. Other teams have a very limited life span, being pulled together to accomplish a specific task and then disbanded. Some teams are relatively informal, meeting occasionally to resolve unusual problems that arise. Some, like continuous improvement teams or quality circles, are added to the employees' regular duties. Others are very high profile, charged with major one-off tasks that are 'life or death' for the company.

Teams vary considerably, not only in the scope of work assigned to them and its potential impact, but also in the extent to which the team itself rather than someone else in the company establishes goals, allocates resources and is held responsible for results. Some examples:

- A construction crew is a team. Its scope of responsibility is limited, and typically its work has little impact outside the group. It has little control over the resources assigned to it or its work assignments.
- Another kind of team is a project team. Sometimes the team leader estimates and requests resources for the project; sometimes he or she can specify who will be on the team. Projects vary in terms of their budget, complexity of the work, length of time to complete, size of the team. Usually some higher level of management sets the goals and defines the scope of the work.
- A self-managed (or semi-autonomous) work team is one that has considerable authority to make all decisions regarding the team: selection of members, how to do the work, setting team goals and how to use the money allocated to them. Business process teams may fall into this category.

Teams coordinate work because by its nature a team is a group of highly interacting people who cooperate to produce common outcomes. The members see and talk to one another as they work together, and each individual consciously adjusts his or her own activities when needed to mesh with the work of other team members.

Control is achieved in teams because the visible nature of each team member's work both (a) motivates people to meet the team's expectations of performance and (b) provides ample opportunity for other team members to suggest changes. Peer approval and disapproval are powerful influences in leading people to meet expectations.

Teams are especially valuable if:

- You need the input and collaboration of people representing different departments, professional or technical disciplines and points of view.
- Interdependence among tasks is high.
- You would like to have people 'cross-trained' in different skills and abilities. Working on a team, for example, can help a design engineer and a sales representative to understand each other's problems and opportunities.
- The challenges you face are too complex for any one person either to meet or to evaluate a response proposed by someone else.
- Direct interaction among individuals is the fastest and most effective way to coordinate the pieces of work in a project or process.
- You want to encourage employee participation.

A team *works best* when:

- Team members are sufficiently skilled and experienced to do the work and make the necessary decisions.
- Team members have the 'human relations' skill to work well together and are willing to set aside individual preferences when necessary to get results.
- It receives clear goals and direction from management; generally, these should relate to expected results, not to team process.
- After making expectations clear, management is willing to trust the team – to give it time to get established and to provide support when things don't go as planned.

Team spirit

Much has been written about team spirit – that feeling of dedication to the team and enthusiasm about reaching its goals.

Team spirit can be wonderful when:

- It helps highly productive people to produce high-quality goods and services.
- It builds loyalty and commitment to the company as a whole.
- It makes people happy to come to work.

Team spirit is *not* so wonderful when:

- The team becomes more committed to its own goals than to the company's.
- 'Groupthink' develops. It becomes difficult for an individual member to challenge the group, so dissent is silenced.
- Team members become blind to, or just refuse to acknowledge, one another's shortcomings. ('He's one of us so we won't criticise.')

These potential drawbacks can be addressed by having a periodic changeover of team members; however, too frequent changes in membership can prevent or reduce cohesion in the team. The trick is to get a good balance of stability and change and to make sure that team members have access to new ideas and methods.

Points to ponder
1. Think of a team you've been a part of that has achieved particularly good results. Which of the organisational factors discussed above might have contributed to this?
2. How about a team that got poor results? What organisational factors might have led to its failure?

Management style

Management style refers to the way that supervisors and managers interact with the employees who report to them. Style is an aspect of management behaviour that has a big impact on how effective supervisors are likely to be in carrying out their duties. Management style can also affect and be affected by organisation design.

Management style range along a continuum from very high to very low control. At the one extreme, there is the militaristic 'command and control' style where the boss calls the shots and workers have little to say about what or how work gets done.

At the other extreme, there is the completely 'hands off' style where workers themselves decide what work needs to be done and how to do it. In between, there are styles with varying degrees of management control and worker involvement.

One well-known approach to leadership style suggests that the appropriate management style moves between 'telling', 'selling', 'participating', and 'delegating'. As you might guess:

- *Telling* means directing and closely monitoring workers' activities.
- *Selling* means explaining decisions and answering questions.
- *Participating* means joining in discussion with workers to sort out what needs to be done and how.
- *Delegating* means leaving decisions and implementation up to the workers.

Each of these styles involves significantly different behaviours and attitudes in supervisors and workers. In general, the more capable and mature workers are, the more supervisors can use the participation and delegation styles. Conversely, the less able and mature workers are, the more selling and telling styles are needed. Also, in general, the more support workers need to consider and be motivated to do the work, the more participation and selling are appropriate.

Today, another style is being stressed: the *coaching* or *developmental* style. With this approach, the supervisor's objective is to help people understand how best to get their work done; develop the knowledge, abilities and maturity to participate at a higher level; and become more independent or autonomous.

Historically, the telling and selling styles have been most common, especially when the organisation used supervision or standardisation of process as control techniques.

But times are changing. Competition is global now and the

fast pace of change means that the organisation needs all the help it can get from employees at all levels. Being responsive to customers and keeping costs low call for a unified effort – with cooperation, dedication and initiative on the part of every employee.

As a result, the participating, delegating and coaching styles are increasingly favoured. These styles fit particularly well with the coordination and control techniques of standardised outcomes, teams and employee commitment. However, in practice, all the coordination and control techniques we describe can be used with the whole range of management styles.

Points to ponder
Supervision as a control technique can be used with a variety of management styles. What situations are you aware of, in your organisation or elsewhere, where supervisors with different management styles get quite different results?

Informal organisation

So far, we have discussed formal ways to coordinate and control work. But in fact, a lot of coordination and control occurs in quite informal and unofficial ways. Workers often bypass official channels of communication and bend standard operating procedures. This is why it's important to be aware of how things are *actually* done in addition to knowing how they're *supposed* to be done.

Flouting the rules can be harmful if it occurs through ignorance, indifference or even deliberate insubordination. But there are many situations where employees ignore the rules because it is faster and more effective to do so. When you find that formal procedures are regularly ignored in certain situations, it's important to understand why.

If *formal* procedures appear to be appropriate, perhaps employees don't understand them or your current techniques for controlling work are not effective.

- If you rely on *supervision*, perhaps the supervisor is overspanned or needs coaching in how to manage people.
- If you use *standardised process* or *outcomes*, perhaps the standards aren't being clearly communicated. Maybe oral instructions need to be written. Or written manuals are poorly designed and worded. Maybe workers need some training.

If *informal* procedures seem to be more effective than formal ones:

- Involve employees in proposing new formal procedures.
- Review the proposed new procedures with people who will be affected by them – inside and outside the organisation, including customers, if appropriate.
- If the new procedures meet with approval, implement them – at least on a trial basis.

You might also consider reviewing your coordination and control techniques. Maybe there are too many formal rules and procedures. Maybe employees should be allowed to exercise more discretion in how they do their work than they are formally permitted at present.

Guidelines for choosing coordination and control techniques

Who should be involved?

- *Managers and others who are held responsible for results.* In many cases, managers and supervisors may not have given much thought to how they make sure work is coordinated or controlled. Answering the questions in the Worksheet will help them to decide if their current techniques are the most appropriate ones to use.
- *Employees at all levels.* Employees who do the work have useful information on how coordination and control actually occur. In fact, managers at higher levels sometimes aren't aware of the full extent of the informal ways in which work

gets done. Workers can also give useful input concerning what they need to make sure work is progressing as it should.

'What if' scenario

We'll say that a hypothetical telephone company is considering controlling operators by *outcomes* rather than through *supervision*. They propose using a computer to track all the information the supervisors currently monitor — for example, length of time spent per call, number of calls answered per day, and so on. Their analysis might look like the following.

Change being considered
- Use computer to track outcomes, eliminating the need for supervisors to monitor behaviour.

Potential benefits
- Salary costs will be lower with supervisory positions eliminated.
- Operators will have a more comfortable work environment by not having supervisors constantly looking over their shoulders.
- Operators will develop more personal responsibility for keeping up good performance.

Potential drawbacks
- Although the computerised reports will be available every day, problems with operator performance will be discovered through analysis only after the fact.
- Some operators, particularly if they are inexperienced, may need the guidance of a supervisor when unusual situations arise.

Worksheet

Ask yourselves the following questions.

1. **When do we use the following methods to coordinate work and/or control work?**

    *Supervision*_____

    Standardising process _____

    *Standardising outcomes*_____

    *Standardising inputs*_____

    *Employee commitment*_____

    *Employee teams*_____

2. **Describe any problems that have arisen in your work situation due to the technique used.**

    _____

    _____

    _____

3. **Are there informal coordination and control methods used that sometimes replace the formal methods?** If so, should you consider *enforcing* the formal methods? How about *changing* the formal methods?

    _____

    _____

    _____

4. **Think of your new organisation structure (or one that you would like to implement). What would be the most appropriate techniques for coordinating and controlling work in different parts of your organisation?** Keep in mind how the new structure may have

changed spans of control, interdependencies, the nature of the work, and so on.

_____

_____

_____

5. For each change proposed in 4. above, think through a 'what if' scenario, identifying the potential benefits and costs of making the change in technique. (See the 'What If' box for an example of this.)

6. Before actually implementing changes, especially if they are major, be sure to get input from the people who are responsible for the results of the work as well as the people who do the work.

CHAPTER 5

Measuring Performance

The purpose of measuring performance is to see whether you're getting the results you want and, if not, where adjustments need to be made. People pay attention to what's being measured. Measurement can be both a motivator and a threat. Some would argue that, though often used to focus on instances of failure, measurement is most powerful when used to focus on instances of success. Certainly, you'll get the most out of any performance measurement system if you spend at least as much time reinforcing good performance as trying to correct poor performance.

Performance measurement consists of four basic steps:

1. *Deciding what to measure*, and how often
2. *Setting standards* or criteria for performance
3. *Noting any deviations* from the standards
4. Determining when and how to *take corrective action*.

What to measure?

People pay attention to what gets measured, so be sure to measure those results you really need to keep track of. To help you decide which results these are, think about your:

- *Goals* – the concrete results you intend to accomplish within a certain period

- *Key success factors* – those things you must do on an ongoing basis to be successful
- *Business processes* – key milestones in your business processes.

Most companies have measures that relate to financial results, costs of production, quantity and quality of goods produced, individual employee performance and customer satisfaction. For example:

> *Beaumont Machining attracts and retains customers by promising high-quality work, not necessarily at the lowest price. They make a high margin of profit on each order. They measure performance on two critical success factors: (1) quality of the product (accurate machining, durable materials, attractive finish); and (2) timeliness – that is, meeting promised delivery dates. (They have other performance measures also.)*

> *Enlok Windows, by contrast, faces a highly competitive market where they must often be willing to lower their profit in order to make a sale. Their goals and measures are related to (1) volume – that is, total sales per year, and (2) production costs per order. The more they can sell and the more they can keep costs down, the more profit they will make.*

These are some of the most common aspects of performance that get measured, with examples of the kind of measures used for each.

- **Profitability**. This refers to how much money is made after expenses – or the extent to which revenues exceed costs.
  Measures: Net sales (total value of sales minus cost of producing the goods or services). Earnings per share of stock. Return on assets.

- **Competitiveness**. The extent to which your organisation is succeeding against competitors.
  Measures: Percentage of market share or your total volume of sales for a certain product as a percentage of total volume of sales for that product by all producers.

- **Efficiency**. Accomplishing results with the least wasteful use of resources.
  Measures: Resources expended per unit of output. Processing time per unit produced. Average number of customers served or units produced per employee. Average length of downtime of machinery or facilities.

- **Effectiveness**. Doing the right things to meet your customer's needs.
  Measures: Number of repeat customers. Ratings on customer satisfaction survey where customers are asked what their needs are and to what extent your products and services meet these needs.

- **Quality**. This refers to meeting or exceeding specifications or requirements.
  Measures: Percentage of products meeting quality criteria. Number of customer compliments or complaints. Number of product rejects. Ratings on customer satisfaction survey.

- **Volume**. This refers to quantity of output.
  Measures: Number of products manufactured, despatched, sold. Number of customers served, projects completed.

- **Innovation**. The extent to which you produce new ideas or adapt old ideas to create profitable results.
  Measures: Number of patents obtained for products. Number of new products or services developed. Number of employee suggestions implemented. Amount of money saved through continuous improvement of work processes.

- **Quality of work life**. This refers to aspects of the work environment that are valued by employees.
  Measures: Ratings on employee satisfaction survey. Employee turnover and absenteeism rates. Number of workplace accidents.

Process or outcomes?

Always measure outcomes – even when you don't want to be too specific about what results should be. This would be the case, for instance, in a group trying to develop a new computer game.

The total quality movement of the last few decades stresses the importance of doing things right the first time rather than having to redo them because the end product is flawed. One way to ensure this is to have inspections and measurements at different stages in the process.

Incidentally, note that measuring the process doesn't necessarily imply having a standardised process. Having a standardised process means workers are told how to perform each step of the task. By contrast, measuring the process means that results at various stages are specified and then measured.

In brief, measure process as well as outcome when:

- There is a clear connection between how each step in the process is done and the final outcome
- It is likely mistakes may be made along the way – because the process is particularly complicated or variable, workers are inexperienced and so on
- Getting interim measurements will enable you to make corrections early and avoid flaws in the final product or service.

Points to ponder

Employees sometimes find it threatening to have their work results measured. How might you overcome their fears?

Setting standards for measurement

Deciding *what* to measure is often considerably easier than deciding *how* to measure it and what an acceptable standard should be. For example, you may decide that you need to measure quality, and that one measure of good quality would be the number of rejects. But what is an acceptable number of rejects? Is it realistic to expect zero rejects?

Beaumont Machining established 'number of rejects' as a measure of quality and 'number of times the promised delivery date is met' as a measure of timeliness. The company's desire is to get zero rejects and always meet every promised delivery date. However, for reasons that are often beyond its control, this is not always possible. So the supervisor and machinists jointly decided on the following minimum standards:

Reject rate: *less than 5 per cent.*
Timeliness: *promised delivery dates met for 80 per cent of orders; within 48 hours for remaining orders.*

Performance is measured once a month. If standards are not met, the supervisor, workers and sometimes the owner also, meet to determine what is causing the problems and try to correct the situation.

Two important questions to ask are how often and under what conditions should you do the measurement. For example, it seems sensible to measure the quality of products by examining a few examples coming off one machine at the same time every day. However, when you do this, you tend to observe products under the same conditions every time — same workers, same hour of the shift, same machine, same amount of machine running time. It's unwise to assume that the measure of quality you get at this one time, on this one machine, will hold for all times and machines. So, to get an accurate overall picture, you need to measure quality at different times with different workers, different machines, and so on. The same point holds true for all measurements when you want to be able to draw general conclusions, whether about employees, products, services or customers.

Once you decide what aspects of performance to track, how to measure each and under what conditions, you can set up the actual measurement system. You need to answer such questions as: Who will do the measuring? How often? How will they keep track — through a log book, a computer program or other means? Who will compile and report the results?

Measuring qualitative data

It is fairly easy to find ways to measure something that can be *quantified*. It is relatively simple, for instance, to measure value of goods sold in a given period, number of telephone calls answered, number of customer complaints received, number of rejects, length of time to complete task. It is not nearly so easy to measure *qualitative* aspects of performance, such as effective management style, the productivity of administrative employees or the creativeness of engineers, designers and others whose job it is to produce original ideas.

A common way to quantify an abstract concept, such as customer satisfaction, is to do a *survey*. This means, for example, you would ask customers to complete a questionnaire that asks them to rate how well you're doing on various dimensions. If the questionnaire is carefully developed to make sure that the really important aspects of service are covered, this can be a good solution.

It's difficult, however, to avoid introducing a subjective bias into the answers. Consider the following questions asked by one large company in their Quality of Service Evaluation, administered annually. (Customers were asked to circle a number from 1 to 5, with 1 representing poor and 5 representing excellent.)

How do our services compare in terms, cost, quality, value and timeliness with those that could be purchased from other sources?

Please rate the courtesy, cooperation and professionalism of our service representative.

In the case of the first question, obviously the customer's response is going to be affected by how much experience the customer has had with other suppliers. Or the answers could be purely guesswork based on what the customer thinks other suppliers could provide. Similarly, the second question will be biased by the extent to which the person answering the question actually interacts with the service representative and likes him or her.

In spite of these shortcomings, the company feels that over-positive ratings tend to balance out over-negative ones, and that the results still give useful information on how customers view the service providers. Also, note that, while the survey is concerned with *qualitative* issues, the responses can be *quantified*. This makes it easy to track results over time and compare the results of one group with another.

Acting on results

Keeping in mind that measures are tools to help you improve performance, it is clear that what you do with the results is as important as deciding what and how to measure. Once the results are in, the next steps are to:

1. Determine what deviations occur – that is, where results exceed or fall below what is expected.
2. Communicate the information to everyone involved in producing the results.
3. Use this information to reinforce good performance and correct poor performance.

If results *meet or exceed expectations*, be sure to acknowledge the workers responsible and, if appropriate, have them explain their success to other workers.

If results fall *below expectations*, you need to find out why. Focus on the problem itself, rather than trying to pin the blame on people. Don't punish people for telling the truth. We've all heard of situations where the boss has a tendency to 'shoot the messenger' who is delivering the bad news. This practice has two unfortunate consequences.

- Workers spend time and energy defending themselves against accusations of blame, rather than trying to understand and resolve the problem causing the poor performance.
- Workers are sometimes tempted to 'fudge' the data to ensure that they have good results to report. For example, a bad run of widgets might get written off as an aberration and not be included in the day's numbers. Or only those

customers who do a lot of business with the company, and thus get special treatment, are asked about their satisfaction with the company's services.

In both situations, measurement is not being used as the helpful tool it can be in improving performance.

No matter whether results exceed or fall short of standards, it's important to review the standards at regular intervals to see if they need to be revised. Sometimes this decision will be driven by your competition. For example, if a competitor starts to produce the same product you sell – at the same price but higher quality – you may have to raise your quality standards, even if your workers are finding it difficult to meet the current standards.

Communicating results, whatever they are, should be done frequently so that people know how they're doing as they go along. This enables problems to be corrected in a timely way. Many companies have an annual review of performance, both for individual workers and for the company as a whole. However, a year is a long time to wait to find out what's going well and what needs to be changed.

To be most effective, a *measurement–feedback–correction* cycle should be an integral part of the work so that workers find it easy to check their performance regularly and be essentially self-correcting.

Measurement pitfalls

Two major pitfalls to avoid are 'measuring everything to death' and 'over-concern with measurement'.

Too many measures
This situation occurs when a company is too conscientious, and possibly too unselective, in what it measures. It seems that everything that can be quantified is measured. Worse still, as yet more things need to be tracked, new measures are added without any old ones being dropped.

You can guess what happens. People stop being diligent

about collecting the data, so often the resulting reports are inaccurate. As a result, those people who are supposed to monitor the results don't do it as much. If there are some conscientious people who really do track everything they're supposed to, they end up spending more time on measuring the work than in doing the work. Here are some ways to avoid the 'too many measures' pitfall:

- Concentrate on what's really important to the survival and growth of your business. Refer back to your goals, key success factors and business processes. Get input from your customers to help you set priorities.
- Don't give in to the temptation to measure something just because it's easy to measure. Measuring unimportant things dilutes the attention paid to important things.
- Limit the number of things you measure. Some experts suggest having no more than ten measures of performance.

Take a look at all the things you measure regularly and ask: Why are we measuring this? Who actually uses the information, and how does it affect what our company does? Does anything change as a result? What would happen if we simply dropped this measure?

Over-concern with measurement

Measurement is important, but not more so than being responsive to customers or doing the work well. However, it is possible for an organisation, and for individuals, to become so carried away with racking up a high score on some aspects of performance that they overlook other – even more critical – aspects.

This situation is largely an unintended consequence of rewarding good performance! So if an employee is rewarded for exceeding measurement standards on quality criteria, this is what he or she will focus on, and other, unmeasured, aspects of performance may be ignored.

Consider the following case where a company's priorities changed during the course of the year.

Among several goals set by a software company at the beginning of the year was to develop a software product for a new market, the legal market. The company's existing and highly successful product is a software package for financial managers. Part-way through the year, a competitor introduces a financial package that directly competes with this product. The major concern now becomes to meet this threat in every way it can: whether by adding new features to its financial package, cutting prices for new customers or providing better service for existing customers. The company still wants to develop a legal software package, but this is no longer as urgent a need as meeting the competitive threat to the accounting package.

Quite commonly, especially in large companies, when a situation like this occurs, the person or unit responsible for the legal package will still be held to the original goals. They will be measured on their success in achieving these goals. Thus, they will be reluctant to shift their priorities to focus time and resources on meeting the new threat unless the measures of success they are expected to meet are changed accordingly.

Here's a hypothetical example that illustrates a situation where what is *not* measured may be as important to the company in the long run as what *is*.

Two managers at year's end claim they have each achieved cost reductions of £15,000 during the year for their respective departments; quality of work results remained the same. The managers received the same bonus for good performance.

Does this mean that the performance for the two departments is identical? Not necessarily. In one department, at year's end, employees expressed enthusiasm about their work, satisfaction with the company, their manager and the work environment. In the other department, dissatisfied employees were seeking employment elsewhere. Clearly, some things are working better in the first department than the second, and the manager of the first department is probably more effective than the manager of the second. But whatever the first manager is doing right is not being measured at present.

Points to ponder

Because most organisations try to limit the number of performance measures, some aspects of performance are often not measured.

1. Can you think of instances where important aspects of performance are not measured?
2. How can you compensate for this omission?

Guidelines for developing performance measures

Who should be involved?

- *Top management.* What to measure is directly related to goals and key success factors, so top management should be involved in deciding, or at least in approving, what gets measured and how.
- *Middle- and first-level supervisors* who set goals and success factors for their own units similarly must decide, or at least approve, what is measured in their units.
- *Other employees* who have to do the measuring. They'll know what it makes sense to measure and how easy or difficult it will be to get the data. Also, if people participate in decisions on what and how to measure, they are more likely than non-participants to be committed to carrying out those decisions.
- *Other stakeholders* who will be affected by the results. These include other units within the company that your unit interacts with in carrying out work, and customers and others outside the company. Customers especially can provide valuable information on what aspects of performance they value and what their priorities are; for example, whether they value timeliness more than low cost, durability more than appearance of the product, and so on.

Worksheet

Ask the following questions.

1. **What aspects of performance do you wish to measure – quality, quantity, cost, others?**

   _____

   _____

   _____

2. **Prioritise the above. Are they critical to your business? Nice to have but not critical?**

   _____

   _____

   _____

3. **What are measures of each of these?**

   _____

   _____

   _____

4. **From 2. and 3., prepare a list of all the measures you'd like to track.** Answer the following questions for each one.

   - Is it really important to our business to have this measure?
   - What would happen if we dropped it?
   - Are we including any measures just because they're easy to get?
   - Are there important aspects of performance we left off our list just because they're difficult to measure? If so, should we make a special effort to develop measures for them?

- Who will use the information we gather from these measures, and what will they do with it?
- Is this information likely to help us improve performance (or put the blame on individuals)?

5. **The above analysis may lead you to add or drop some measures on your list. Review the measures that remain, and for each one determine:**

- How will the data be collected – through a computer program, logbook, machine count or other?
- Who will collect the data – supervisors, workers, administrative assistants, others?
- How often will data be collected – daily, weekly, monthly or for each task as it's completed?
- Who will compile and report the results, and how frequently?
- Who will communicate the results? To whom?
- What is the process for making sure that results are acted on?

6. **Decide at what intervals you will review measurement systems.**

CHAPTER 6
Putting the Pieces Together

Now that you have worked through the major pieces of a new organisation design, it's time to put them together, stand back and look at the whole.

We suggest you gather your notes – including any charts, descriptions and organised lists – from each of the preceding chapters. It's helpful to display organisation charts and lists of issues so that you can see them all at once. If your organisation is small to medium-sized, you may be able to create one chart that shows all the boxes and lines. If your organisation is large, you may need to examine your design in sections.

Implementing the changes

Having spent time, money and effort in designing your organisation, it's important that you now pay equal attention to seeing that the new organisation is well implemented. We will briefly touch on three particularly important facets of implementation. These are *communication, impact analysis* and *transition management*.

Communication
You are off to a head start if you have involved relevant stakeholders throughout the design process. This means there are people who will already understand some things about the

design and hopefully have some degree of commitment to making it work. But it probably wasn't possible to involve all the stakeholders all of the time. So the first important part of implementation is to communicate.

What to communicate
The purpose of the communication is to describe the new organisation, how it is different from the old and the reasons for the changes.

- *Employees* will want to know how their jobs will be affected: if they'll be doing different work, reporting to a new supervisor, working with different people or transferred to a new location.
- *Trade unions*, if you have them, will similarly want to know how their members will fare in the change, if work rules are to be altered or any other aspects of the union contract affected.
- *Customers* will want to know if products and services will be different, if they'll be working with different contact people from your organisation or if procedures for handling orders will change.
- *Others outside the organisation* who may be affected will want to know what impact the new organisation has on them. They might include shareholders, suppliers, banks, community groups, and so on.

How to communicate
It's useful to have both written and face-to-face communications. A written communication provides a document that the recipient can refer to at will – while face-to-face settings, such as meetings, enable the audience to interact with the presenters.

Common ways of communicating a new organisation design to employees include the following:

- An organisation-wide meeting in which the new organisation is presented to everyone at once. (In large organisations, this is made possible through the use of modern

technology such as satellite broadcasts; questions from employees at remote locations are submitted by telephone.)
- A 'cascading' series of meetings where each level of management describes the new organisation to their employees.
- Written notices sent to all employees or posted on bulletin boards, on electronic mail, and so on.

To people outside the organisation, methods of communication include:

- Newsletters or annual reports
- Individual meetings (for example, with major suppliers or customers), as appropriate
- Press conferences, shareholder meetings, and so on.

No matter how you choose to communicate, it's important to give people the chance to raise questions and concerns and, if possible, have these addressed. In fact, this kind of two-way communication is critical throughout the entire implementation process.

Impact analysis
Before implementing the new design, it's important to think through the impact any changes will have on other aspects of your organisation − the 'ripple effects'. This is important in three ways. First, it helps you to identify what needs to be done to implement the new organisation. Second, it helps you to anticipate and manage disruptions in the work that may occur during implementation. Third, it will uncover resistance or active opposition to the new design.

To arrive at a list of issues you'll need to resolve, consider holding a brainstorming session with people inside the organisation and some of those outside the organisation who are likely to be affected. In particular, if different steps of key business processes occur in different parts of the company, be sure to involve representatives of every step in your brainstorming session.

If you had earlier made a decision to design an 'ideal'

organisation, leaving aside the needs and talents of existing employees, now is the time to consider how current employees will fit into the proposed organisation – and whether the proposed design should be modified to accommodate your current workforce, facilities or other resources.

There are many issues that generally come up in an impact analysis. Some of the major ones are:

- *Personnel.* Can the staffing needs of your proposed organisation be filled with existing employees? Will there be recruitment or lay-offs? Will some people have to be transferred to other jobs, or other locations? Will training be needed for different duties? Is morale likely to suffer? (It often does, especially when jobs are lost or changed.)
- *Trade unions.* If you have many unionised employees, will working practices be affected? If so, how will you negotiate with the unions?
- *Space and equipment.* Will new or different office or plant space be required? New or different tools and equipment? New office technology, such as computers or telephones?
- *Costs.* What will be the costs of making these changes in terms of salaries, training, changes in space or equipment?
- *Productivity.* Will productivity be affected during the changeover? (It often dips when changes of any kind are made.) What arrangements will you make to monitor and minimise this effect?
- *Systems.* Will you need to develop new systems – for example, for job appraisals, remuneration, management information, measuring performance?
- *Communication channels.* Will customers, suppliers, regulators or other stakeholders have to communicate with your organisation in different ways?

Presenting the information
Once you've identified the issues, appoint a person or group to examine each issue or set of issues and make recommendations on how to proceed. Their findings will be relevant to the

implementation schedule. Also, they may recommend that some parts of the proposed design be modified or postponed for consideration at another time.

Transition management

Once an impact analysis is completed, you'll have an understanding of some of the things that need to be managed in making the transition to the new organisation.

The more wide-ranging the changes you're planning to make, the more important it is to have a *transition plan*. This would lay out the steps involved in moving from the old to the new organisation, who is responsible for doing what and the timing of each event.

In a large organisational change affecting many people, you may wish to appoint a *transition coordinator* or *transition manager* to oversee the changes and possibly have a *transition team* to assist this person. (Incidentally, in terms of organisation design, this would be a 'project team' with an assigned task of limited duration.)

This coordinator and team would help address such questions as:

- How is existing work to be handled while the organisation is in transition?
- Do employees need guidance to close down their previous work assignments before moving to new assignments?
- Will old and new organisations co-exist for a time, with the latter being phased in gradually? Or will there be an official 'changeover day' with all changes being made at one time?
- How will you keep track of changes to ensure the new organisation is actually implemented as planned? And to make sure that it is working as efficiently and effectively as you had anticipated?

Key success factors and design

The 'ideal' design alternative for one key success factor might be quite different from the ideal alternative for another factor. Since trade-offs are inevitable, you may be able to organise around the most critical success factor and find other ways to ensure that the others are addressed.

Different success factors may be operable at different times. Also, it is quite appropriate to respond to the needs of different parts of the organisation in different ways. For example, an organisation may have both a research and development (R&D) department and a manufacturing department with quite different success factors and corresponding different design needs.

Key success factors for R&D may be to keep ahead of competitors technologically and build initiative and creativity in employees. The best design alternatives might, therefore, be a flat structure with broad spans of control. Employee commitment and broadly specified outcomes may be the best means of coordination and control.

On the other hand, the key success factor for manufacturing may be keeping production costs low. Thus, this department would probably want more centralised decision making, with standardisation of both process and outcomes.

Table 6.1 on pages 111–12 lists examples of common success factors and indicates which aspects of organisation design it is appropriate to consider for each. The design alternatives shown should be treated as a *starting point only*. It's important to refer to the full discussion in the relevant chapters to see under what conditions each alternative would work best, what the potential drawbacks are and what other alternatives may be better in your own situation.

Review of major issues

Whatever the size of your organisation, or however broad or narrow the scope of your design efforts, it will be helpful to think through the major issues one more time.

1. *Do your organisation's mission, goals and key success factors capture what your business is about and what you need to do to succeed? Do the business processes you've identified match your mission and goals?*

Table 6.1. *Key success factors and organisation design*

Key success factor	Design alternatives to consider
Efficiency – low costs of production	*Work structure.* Functional organisation promotes economies of scale by having similar work done in same place. Business process teams lower costs of coordination across functions.
	Management structure. Centralised decision making can help to control costs.
	Coordination and control. All techniques could work. Think about standardised processes, teams, employee commitment.
Effectiveness – understanding and responding to customers' needs	*Work structure.* Customer-based or business process teams.
	Management structure. Decentralised decision making, flat structure.
	Coordination and control. Employee commitment, teams, standardised outcomes.
Technological leadership	*Work structure.* Product-based or functional.
	Management structure. Decentralised decision making with respect to technological decisions.
	Coordination and control. Supervision with participating, delegating or coaching styles; broadly specified outcomes, employee commitment.
High quality work and products (accuracy, durability, etc)	*Work structure.* Business process teams, functional or product-based.
	Management structure. Any could work.
	Coordination and control. Standardised process with measurement at interim steps in the work process, and standardised outcomes are commonly used. Teams, employee commitment and supervision can also work.

Table 6.1. *Key success factors and organisation design (cont.)*

Key success factor	Design alternatives to consider
Fast turnaround or cycle time	*Work structure.* Business process teams. *Management structure.* Flat, decentralised decision making. *Coordination and control.* Teams, standardised outcomes, supervision.
Flexibility and efficiency in allocating resources	*Work structure.* Matrix. *Management structure.* Centralised decision making for company-wide flexibility. *Coordination and control.* Any, but especially teams, employee commitment.
Employee initiative and creativity	*Work structure.* Business process and customer-based structures promote customer service. Product-based and functional structures promote new technology development. *Management structure.* Flat, broad spans of control, decentralised decision making. *Coordination and control.* Employee commitment, standardised outcomes.
Broadening employee skills	*Work structure.* Matrix, business process. *Management structure.* Flat, broad spans of control, decentralised decision making. *Coordination and control.* Standardised outcomes, teams, employee commitment.

Note. Treat these design alternatives as a starting point only. Please refer to the relevant chapters for a full discussion of their use and potential drawbacks.

The mission and goals of your organisation define what you're trying to achieve, your basic direction. These, combined with your particular business situation, determine your key success factors — the things you must do to be successful. It's important to be clear about all three because the design of your organisation can help or hinder you in achieving them.

Understanding your business processes helps you to see

where there are critical interdependencies in the work and where you need coordination.

2. *Does the way you've divided the work into units such as divisions and departments support your business process?*

No matter how work is divided – whether by function, product, customer, and so on – the structure should help you to carry out your business processes. For example, highly interdependent steps in each business process should be located close to each other so that coordination and control of those steps is easier.

3. *Is your management structure appropriate for the control and coordination you need to carry out your business processes? Does it match the degree of independence, knowledge and skill your employees can exercise in doing their work?*

You need enough levels of management to handle the tasks of coordinating and controlling work, but not so many that they get in the way of making effective and efficient use of your resources. Some decisions will need to be centralised, while others will serve customers better and contribute more to the success of your company if they are decentralised.

4. *Do the methods of control and coordination you have selected provide the right mix of reliance on employees to do the right thing and on managers to ensure that the right thing is done?*

You will probably use a mix of supervision and standardisation to control and coordinate work. In addition, if your company is like many others, you'll be increasingly exploring the use of teams and relying, to some extent at least, on employee commitment to make sure the right work is done the right way.

In general, it's a good idea to delegate to employees as much responsibility and authority as they can handle – or maybe just a touch more than they are comfortable with if you want them to develop more knowledge and initiative. (In the latter case, good management or team support should be available.)

Finally, it's important to keep track of performance through the use of appropriate measurement systems, and to use the results both to discover and correct the sources of poor performance and to discover and reward the sources of good performance.

Conclusion

The design of your organisation is not carved in stone. Indeed, because organisations today face unprecedented competition and unpredictable markets, they need to be more finely attuned than ever to their customers and to changing business conditions.

The key to continued success is to have a firm enough organisational structure to guide productive activity and provide stability, but also a flexible enough structure that you can change to meet the changing needs of your business environment. As the old saying goes, 'the only constant is change'. We all might as well develop the knowledge and skills to handle it.

There is no cut and dried formula for arriving at organisation design decisions. Every alternative you choose will involve trade-offs. You may, for example, want the high level of expertise a functional structure fosters, combined with the quick responsiveness to customers that is better served by a horizontal (business process) structure. The solution is to pick what you think is the best all-round alternative and find ways to make up for potential weaknesses in your choice. If you have thought through the 'Points to ponder' questions in this book, you may already have found ways to overcome or lessen the effects of many design drawbacks.

One cautionary note: it's important not to get carried away by all the latest management buzzwords and fads. While there is much value in many of the latest recipes for success, some involve 'old wine in new bottles'. The fundamental issues in structuring an organisation remain very much the same as they have been for many decades.

We hope this book helps you to make your choices and get good results from doing so.

Glossary

Accountability   The state of being held answerable for results.

Authority   The right to make decisions about what others do and how they do it, how much money to spend on what, and so on.

Autonomy   In a work setting, having control over one's activities and relative freedom from supervision.

Business process   The sequence of tasks and activities that must be completed to provide a product or service to the customer.

Centralised/Decentralised   How concentrated or dispersed the authority to make decisions is.

Chain of command   See *Management hierarchy*.

Competitors, competition   People or companies outside the organisation who seek to capture the same customers.

Control   Making sure the right work is getting done in the right way, and instigating corrective action if expected results are not achieved.

Coordination   Linking together the activities of individuals and/or organisational units to produce a desired outcome − for example, a product or service.

Core business process   A business process that is directly related to the organisation's mission.

Cross-functional team   A team whose members represent different functions or units.

Culture, corporate   The set of shared attitudes, values and behaviours that characterise an organisation.

Customer   Anyone who uses the products or services of an organisation. Usually called a client where professional services are provided – for example, by a lawyer or consultant. (In this book, we use the term *customer* to refer to anyone who receives goods or services from an organisation.)

Customer-based structure   A structure that forms units according to the characteristics or location of its customers or markets.

Delegation of authority   The situation where a person with authority to make certain decisions formally transfers that authority to subordinates.

Division of labour   Separation of work into tasks that can be done by different people or organisational units.

Economies of scale   The savings obtained in cost and time when a large number of similar activities or products is processed at the same time, by the same equipment, in the same place or by the same people.

Effectiveness   Getting desired results or doing what will meet the customer's needs.

Efficiency   Accomplishing results with the least wasteful use of resources.

Employee   In our usage, everyone who draws a pay cheque from an organisation. This term thus encompasses both managers and workers.

Employee commitment   Employee dedication to the success of the organisation. Usually implies a strong belief in the values and goals of the organisation.

Employee involvement   The practice of involving employees in solving problems and making decisions.

Environment, business   Political, economic and competitive conditions outside the organisation that have an impact on the organisation. These include major political or natural events; new technology; demographic shifts; and the actions and attitudes of customers, governments, competitors, pressure groups and community organisations.

First-level management   The managers who directly supervise workers – the lowest level of management (also commonly called *first-level supervisor*).

Flat structure   An organisation structure with relatively few levels between the highest management level and the worker level.

Flowcharting   See *Workflow charting*.

Functional structure   A structure that has units formed according to major technical or professional function performed — for example, *Sales, Engineering.*

Goals Concrete results that the organisation intends to achieve within a specified period.

Headcount The number of employees in an organisation's workforce.

Horizontal structure A structure based on business process teams. It is called horizontal because the work units cut across traditional functions rather than relying on a vertical hierarchy to coordinate activity.

Hybrid organisation An organisation that has a mix of structural forms. For example, it may be product-based at the highest level, with functional departments within each product division.

Impact analysis An analysis conducted prior to implementing an organisation change. Its purpose is to determine how the proposed new organisation design will affect existing structures, systems, people and results.

Implementation The process of putting into practice a plan, design, strategy or idea.

Influence The ability to affect what others do or believe, regardless of whether one has the authority to do so.

Informal organisation Unofficial procedures and channels of communication regularly used by employees.

Informational systems Typically, computer-based systems to collect, organise and display information useful to the business.

Inputs Resources that are fed into a work process. These include the skills and knowledge of people, information, materials and so on.

Interdependence The extent to which two or more steps or tasks depend on one another. For example, the outcome of one step is the input for the next step, or a mistake made in one step will lead to flawed results in the next step.

Job A relatively stable cluster of activities and responsibilities assigned to one person.

Key success factors Something an organisation must do well in order to be successful — for example, *keep costs low* or *respond quickly to customer requests.*

Management hierarchy The ordering of people and work in levels, one above the other. The people at each level supervise those in the level below them. The bottom level in an organisation consists of workers who do not supervise others.

Management structure   Reflects the way managers are distributed throughout the organisation, in terms of the hierarchy or number of levels of management, spans of control and the centralisation or decentralisation of decision making.

Management style   The way that managers interact with people at lower levels in the organisation – in particular, how much control the manager exerts or how much autonomy employees are permitted.

Manager   Someone who is responsible for directing, coordinating and controlling the work.

Market   The field of action where goods and services are bought and sold.

Matrix structure   A structure where individuals simultaneously report to two or more supervisors.

Measuring performance   The process of gathering information about outcomes produced by people or organisations.

Middle management   The levels of management between the top level (chief executive officer and those reporting directly to him/her) and the first-level managers who directly supervise workers.

Mission   The ongoing purpose of an organisation, or the reason it exists.

Motivation   Something that causes a person to behave in a certain way. Positive motivational factors include rewards such as salary, interesting work, dedication to the company's success.

Non-core process   A work process that does not directly affect the organisation's mission.

Organisation   Any collection of people or activities formed for a specific purpose. The purpose can be to make money, as with most business organisations, or to accomplish other purposes – such as charity, recreation, political action, education, worship and so on.

Organisational chart   A chart that displays how the work of an organisation is divided up into 'boxes' (divisions, departments and so on) and who reports to whom (the 'lines').

Organisation design   Planning and fitting together the people and activities in an organisation.

Outcomes   The results of work activity, such as products and services. This term is often used interchangeably with *outputs* or *results*.

Performance   Describes the results accomplished by an individual or organisation, often in comparison with goals, targets or other criteria.

Performance measurement   See *Measuring performance.*

Power   The ability to control the actions and decisions of others even if they resist.

Procedures   Descriptions of how a task or activity is done, often written down in detail.

Product-based structure   A structure that forms units according to products or services delivered to customers – for example, Refrigerator Division, Oven Division, Savings Accounts, Credit Card Accounts.

Productivity   The quantity of products and services delivered divided by the amount of resources (labour, capital, materials, equipment) used. (Total output divided by total input.) Also see *Efficiency.*

Profit centre   A division of an organisation that is evaluated according to the profits it generates. Profit centres can generate their own revenues and make their own business decisions.

Profitability   The extent to which revenues exceed costs.

Quality   The extent to which goods or services meet or exceed expectations or standards.

Re-engineering   The process of completely rethinking and redesigning how an organisation carries out its work.

Regulators   Agencies that impose rules and restrictions on organisations.

Reorganisation   Changing any component of an organisation, including its mission, goals, strategies and structures.

Resources   People, money, materials, technology or anything else that helps the organisation to produce its goods and services.

Restructuring   Changing the structure of an organisation: the way work is divided into units, number of levels of hierarchy, spans of control, and so on.

Self-managing teams   Employee teams who have considerable authority to make decisions concerning the team and its work. These decisions include setting goals, deciding how to do the work, assigning work, allocating resources and selecting team members.

Span of control   Refers to the number of people directly reporting to a manager or supervisor. If there are relatively few people, it is a narrow span of control; if relatively many, it is a broad span of control.

Stakeholder   All those people or institutions who have an interest in an organisation and who can influence its actions and success. Stakeholders include customers, employees, other units, shareholders, suppliers and regulators.

Standardisation   Setting standards and criteria to make sure that events follow a predictable path and produce predictable outcomes. Organisations can standardise work *process, outcomes* of work and *inputs* to the work.

Strategy   A plan for how the organisation will carry out its mission and achieve its goals.

Structure, organisation   Refers to the way that people and activities are clustered and relate to one another as shown on an organisation chart. It includes the way work is divided into units such as divisions and departments, the levels of hierarchy, spans of control, and centralisation or otherwise of decision making.

Subordinates   Non-management employees. We have generally used the term *workers* rather than subordinates.

Success factors   See *Key success factors.*

Supervision   The process of overseeing, coordinating and controlling the activities and outcomes of others.

Survey   A set of questions, administered either verbally or through a written questionnaire, to customers, employees or others to gather information on attitudes, experiences with company products or practices and so on.

System   A set of procedures pertaining to a certain function. For example, a system would prescribe salary levels for different jobs, how salary increases are to be decided, and so on.

Tall structure   A structure with many supervisory levels between top management and worker level.

Task   A specific piece of work.

Team   A group of employees who work together to accomplish a task.

Technology   The scientific knowledge, methods, tools and equipment used to produce goods and services. The term *high technology* refers to the use of sophisticated electronic devices and methods.

Technology-driven   An organisation, market, product or service that develops because of the technology that enables it to exist.

Total quality management (TQM) A movement promoting a collection of ideas and techniques that enables continuous improvement in work processes and the resulting products.

Transition In our usage, refers to the period during which an organisation is changing from its existing design to a new design.

Unit In our usage, any subdivision of an organisation – for example, division, department, team.

Values Deeply held and enduring beliefs about what is good and desirable.

Workers In our usage, refers to employees who do not manage or supervise anyone. (Also referred to as *subordinates*).

Workflow charting Diagramming all the tasks in a work process to delineate the sequence of activities, the inputs to each task and the outputs generated.